Thinking about Thinking

I0809300

ADRIAAN T. PEPERZAK

Thinking about Thinking

WHAT KIND OF CONVERSATION IS PHILOSOPHY?

Fordham University Press
New York 2012

Copyright © 2012 Fordham University Press

All rights reserved. No part of this publication may be reproduced, stored in a retrieval system, or transmitted in any form or by any means—electronic, mechanical, photocopy, recording, or any other—except for brief quotations in printed reviews, without the prior permission of the publisher.

Fordham University Press has no responsibility for the persistence or accuracy of URLs for external or third-party Internet websites referred to in this publication and does not guarantee that any content on such websites is, or will remain, accurate or appropriate.

Fordham University Press also publishes its books in a variety of electronic formats. Some content that appears in print may not be available in electronic books.

Library of Congress Cataloging-in-Publication Data

Peperzak, Adriaan Theodoor, 1929–
Thinking about thinking : what kind of conversation is philosophy? / Adriaan Theodoor Peperzak. — 1st ed.
p. cm.
Includes bibliographical references (p.) and index.
ISBN 978-0-8232-4017-3 (cloth : alk. paper) — ISBN 978-0-8232-4018-0 (pbk. : alk. paper) 1. Philosophy. 2. Philosophy and religion. I. Title.
BD21.P435 2012
101—dc23

2011018516

Printed in the United States of America

14 13 12 5 4 3 2 1
First edition

CONTENTS

PREFACE

Living with philosophy implies many hours of reflection about the conditions and connections of the life one lives and the thinking (or rethinking) one performs. How does the practice of thinking relate to a philosopher's life, and what sort of questions emerge from the alliance between a driven life and thinking thoughts?

The metaphilosophical fragments gathered in this collection present a few aspects of the philosophical practice that deserve special emphasis, given that they do not often receive the attention due to all of philosophy's essential conditions. The selection of perspectives I adopt here does not claim to be exhaustive, nor do I pretend to deduce them as necessary components of a supreme or all-encompassing viewpoint, method, or master plan. Instead, these chapters suggest a more empirical—and thus more existential—approach to some basic questions, which should neither be skipped nor forgotten during further—argumentative, dialectical, speculative, or otherwise logical—meditations. A certain, albeit provisional and incomplete, coherence of the following chapters can be sketched, however, by, for example, connecting all of them to the mutually implicative phenomena of *conversation* (as supported by mutual trust) and *faith* (as the basic form of trust implied in all varieties of dialogue and conversation). While chapters 1 to 6 focus on the dialogical character of philosophy in its thematic and historical operations, particularly emphasizing the contexts of philosophical education, friendship, and twosome intimacy, the role of faith and trust remains largely implicit in them. In chapters 7 to 10, the dialogical character of thought is not silenced, but trust, as communicative trust, and especially its religious dimension, takes center stage. Other commonalities between the ten chapters could be underlined, but their explication would lead to similar configurations of trust-supported dialogue.

The essays published here have been written, revised, and rewritten over the last twenty-five years, with the generous help of many present and past—and much admired—students. I am deeply grateful to all of them, and especially to Catriona Hanley, Aron Reppmann, Laurel Madison, Jean Tan, Marjolein Oele, Aaron Bunch, Stacy Bautista, Maggie Ann Labinski, Bryan Kibbe, Robert Duncan, and Giancarlo Tarantino. All of them have assisted me with unselfish and skillful patience while beautifully realizing indispensable features of an ideal that has continued to fascinate me since Plato seduced me to philosophy. To them this book is dedicated as a token of my gratitude and admiration.

ACKNOWLEDGMENTS

Several chapters of this book grew out of earlier papers that were thoroughly reworked in response to the beneficial critique of students or colleagues, whom I thank for their remarks in the preface.

A few parts of chapter 1 are borrowed from a text with the Hölderlinian title "*Dass ein Gespräch wir sind*," which was presented at a biannual meeting of the *Deutsche Vereinigung für Phänomenologische Forschung* in October 1996 and published in *Der Anspruch des Anderen, Perspektiven phänomenologischer Ethik*, ed. Bernhard Waldenfels and Iris Därmann (München: Fink Verlag, 1998), 17–34.

Chapter 2 grew out of the essay "On the Unity of Systematic Philosophy and History of Philosophy," published in *History and Anti-History of Philosophy*, ed. T. Z. Lavine and V. Tejera (Dordrecht: Kluwer, 1989), 19–31. Reprinted with kind permission from Springer Science+Business Media B.V.

Chapter 3 is the several times revised version of a paper that was presented at a small conference on hermeneutics at Pennsylvania State University, University Park, in July 1986, which was convened by my good, generous, and regretted friend Joseph J. Kockelmans, who edited and published it in *Hermeneutic Phenomenology* (Washington, D.C.: CARP, 1988), 315–330.

Chapter 4 is a revised version of an address given at a graduate students' conference on education, held at Boston College in March 2009.

In chapter 5 I used but modified a text that was presented as Schuwer Lecture in October 2001 at the annual SPEP Conference in Baltimore. The first version was published in *Phenomenology Today, The Schuwer Lectures 1998-2002*, ed. Daniel J. Martino (Pittsburgh, Penn.: Duquesne University Press, 2003), 54–70.

Chapter 6 is a somewhat modified reprint of my contribution to a festschrift for Emilio Brito under the title *Philosophie et Théologie*, ed. E. Gaziaux (Leuven: Peeters, 2007), 539–545.

Chapter 7 incorporates some parts of "Philosophy—A Way of Life?" which was published in *La filosofia come servizio*, a festschrift in honor of Giovanni Ferretti, edited by Robert Mancini and Maurizio Migliori in *Vita e Pensiero* (Torino, 2010), 819–828.

Chapter 8 is a rewritten and expanded version of "The Universality of Catholic Philosophy," published in *Revista Portuguesa de Filosofia* 60 (2004): 813–826.

Chapter 9 offers, with some modifications, a text that was presented at the Colloquium Castelli of January 4–7, 2008, in Rome, and published in *Il Sacrificio. Archivio di Filosofia* 76 (2009): 39–46.

Chapter 10 is a slightly revised version of the opening address given to the International Congress of the Association of Catholic Institutions of Philosophy, held in Mexico City on September 13–15, 2004. See pp. 31–52 of the proceedings, which were edited by Philippe Capelle and published in *La Filosofia como Mediación* (Mexico City: Universidad Iberoamericana, 2007).

Thinking about Thinking

ONE

That We Are a Conversation

SAYING A SAID

Philosophy is sometimes presented as a system of propositions. The fundamental model is then a *legein ti kata tinos*.[1] "Saying something about something" would be paradigmatic of every philosophy. Hegel and other thinkers, however, have pointed out various difficulties inherent to this model. For example, one can ask how we could discuss the totality of beings, *ta panta, ta onta, to pan,* or being itself as *something,* or to say *something* about this *something*. In order to know the totality or being itself as "something," there would have to be something else from which it would differ. Saying something about the totality of being or about being itself would thus presuppose *something else* beyond the totality or being itself that could be predicated of them. What would that be? Hegel concluded from these and similar arguments that the determination of being or the universe must lie in a kind of self-determination through which the inner truth of the totality unfolds and explicates itself, and that the truth of beings is neither a something nor a thesis or ensemble of theses, but nothing else than the comprehensive, self-articulating identity of all determinations.

Such a critique of the view that holds the *legein ti kata tinos* to be the model of all philosophical thought takes aim at the phrase "something about something." Instead, it tries to approach the truth in other ways, whereby propositions play only a subordinate role. The *legein* or "saying" itself, however, is not called into question but taken for granted.[2] Do not all philosophers appropriate it, while reflecting on their theses or questions? Many philosophers are talking, and much is said; we must therefore not only examine what is said but also investigate the formal structures of saying as stating truths or opinions. In doing so, however, we often forget that all saying implies, besides a speaker, someone who is addressed or spoken to. The event of saying, thanks to which the said exists, is addressed by someone to someone who is not the speaker.[3] The formula of the paradigm with which we began must at least be completed by a *tis* (someone) and a *tini* (to someone): *Tis tini legei ti kata tinos,* someone says something about something to someone. What is said exists only as something addressed, i.e., thanks to a speaking or saying that comes from another in order to arrive at someone who thereby is addressed. It implies an oriented event that originates in an addresser who directs it to an addressee.

Does a said allow us to isolate it methodically from the interpersonal event of saying, so that we can determine its peculiar structure without considering its existential dependence on the addressing that links the addresser and the addressee who are involved in it? The philosophical tradition seems to have treated it often as such. In modern philosophy, for example, the history of thought has been interpreted as a succession of isolated systems, each of which unfolded a theory of beings (including social, intersubjective, and individual ones) in their totality. On this view, individual thinkers certainly could profit from their predecessors, react to one another, and suggest better solutions to common problems, but the particular structure of their interaction was hardly thematized. What interested the great thinkers, according to the usual interpretation, was the universality and "intersubjective" verifiability of the theories they developed, and the criterion for their merit was sought in the validity of these theories for every rational ego. The interchangeability of all egos was thus presupposed in the accepted theory of truth.

If it is not possible to isolate the said from the sayer, a revolution in philosophy and metaphilosophy is inevitable. We can then neither determine what philosophy is, nor can we practice philosophy, unless we know how *dicta* and *scripta* (statements and texts) differ from yet are completely dependent upon personal addresses and, by extension, on dialogues and discussions. The realm of philosophy can then no longer be viewed as a pantheon of heroic but isolated individuals or monological systems, which together (as a library) would compose the history of philosophy. If philosophers are necessarily connected by addressing and being addressed, the philosophical tradition is an eventful and ever shifting history of awakening, suggestion, seduction, interruption, responding, struggling, educating, and learning among friends, colleagues, strangers, or enemies.

SOMEONE SAYS SOMETHING ABOUT SOMETHING TO SOMEONE

Does the completed paradigm permit us to understand the historical adventure called "philosophy"? From the perspective of speaking, each statement is addressed to a potential listener. As such, it invites the addressee to take up what is said as a suggestion for agreement, disagreement, or amendment. Saying something to someone urges the listener or reader to answer the speaker with a reply. The kind of the reply cannot be predicted, but every speaking that reaches its receiver necessarily elicits a response. The listener can reject a speaker's invitation, but if he has really heard it, he cannot avoid answering. Pretending that one has not heard the speaker or reacting with (a more or less qualified) silence is still a reply, sometimes even an eloquent one. A reply is unavoidable, even if the listener did not understand what was said (for example, because it was said in a language unknown to or too difficult for him). *That someone speaks and is heard* suffices for the inevitability of a response. Normally, the reply will consist in a speaking by the person who was addressed, but gestures or silence are equally possible. Any response changes the preceding speaker into a listener, who, in turn, responds to the responder.

The structure of saying, which is always a form of addressing that leads to a responding address, takes time. Consequently, philosophical discourse cannot be understood as a thinking that grasps a statement in the *nunc stans* of a comprehensive overview. Discourse is an interplay of addresses and replies, through which persons direct themselves to each other, alternately acting and reacting. Thus, the paradigm contains two fundamental moments: (1) the saying itself as an intersubjective event and (2) what is said as a suggestion "about something." A phenomenology of philosophy must therefore answer the questions: how do the saying and the said arise in philosophy, and how are they intertwined?

How Can the Said Be Resaid? *Hermeneutical Questions about the Past*

Receptivity Everything that is said has a past. No one has anything to say without previously having heard much that already was said. What we say is for the most part a new version of words or texts that before us and around us have been said or written. When we speak, we repeat or transform, but in any case we continue the saids and sayings and the ways of saying that we have already heard or read. We use, continue, and develop a lingual, cultural, and epochal inheritance. Having something to say, then, presupposes receptivity and acceptance, even in philosophy. Thinking, however original it may be, cannot avoid being receptive and—at least partially—repetitive, not only at the beginning of a philosophical career but always. Since thinking implies reflection, it relies on the past that is kept in memory, on new and old surprises of unpredictable experiences, and on our own and others' lives that have already been lived but not yet understood.

Receptivity is not the same as passivity, however. It is an active reaching out that is driven by a desire of approaching truth—if possible, by a closer intimacy than has been reached before. Thinking is not only receptive; it is a highly active form of acceptance: an attentive, interested, welcoming, positively willed opening up to the given that comes to it.

(Self-)Critique What is said is never a mere repetition. Even if one agrees word for word with something that has been said before, everything—the world, the speaker, the circumstances, the addressee, and the meaning of what was said—has changed. What one says is therefore in each case unique. Although most of our statements are unoriginal, they show through their particular, even unique, style (which can be mediocre, dull, ugly, or trivial) that someone has appropriated and therewith personalized them. Every sentence proves that the author has changed a received gift into a thought of her own. An analysis of what is one's own might then reveal much of what the speaker has borrowed from parents, guides, friends, books, fashions, etc., while at the same time disclosing how all these influences have converged into the unique results of the author's said.

The appropriation of what has already been said, as presupposed in each saying, is never a mere repetition of some past; it is also a testing and an evaluation. Indeed, testing is a structural moment of all human experience, not only of critical thinking but also of the most elementary feeling and perception. Every experience is at the same time an experience of something *and a critical experience of this same experience.* As self-experience, every experience of some phenomenon or event is a test and critique of its own perceived or felt quality:[4] "Do I see that thing there correctly?" "This music is beautiful!—but is my taste good enough?" No experience escapes its own evaluation by the very person who experiences it. In philosophy, the experience of a thought and its expression includes the critical weighing of the degree to which that thought and its expression allow the intended reality to display itself without distortion. But how are we able to carry out this "weighing"? That we carry out such self-evaluations, at least in the form of a critically alert caution, cannot be denied; it seems to presuppose that we continually reach out to a better, more authentic, purer truth beyond all that is already said by others and ourselves.

Yet, such a being-toward- or -with- or -in-the-truth does not entail that anyone is capable of adequately formulating the pure and wholly genuine truth.

Individuality Even if we are somehow already "with" or "in" the truth, we still should ask whether we know ourselves in any clear and accurate sense of "knowing." Are we familiar with the truth that determines our living and speaking? Philosophy has taught that truth itself is universal, but have we recognized that each person's irreplaceable individuality is *and is not* as universal as our shared humanity? A universality that fails to recognize the uniqueness and irreplaceability of singular speakers or simply pushes it aside by classifying their singularity as a feature of contingency betrays a most stubborn fact. Do philosophers have eyes only for humanity in its anonymous universality but not for speakers who rise up behind their statements, opinions, and beliefs? But how is it possible to respect each speaker as an irreplaceable individual? The answer to this question is: only by meeting this individual speaker, you, and replying to your speaking. There is no you, however, if we reduce singular humans to being universal objects, exchangeable instances of a universal essence, or just arbitrary examples of a philosophical theory.

The Time of Philosophy Receptivity and originality are two features of a said that presentifies a retrieved past as a suggestion for the addressee's (and possibly also for the addresser's) future.

The return of the past is often emphasized at the expense of originality. Heidegger's statement that "language speaks,"[5] for instance, is a misleading exaggeration, though it may be justified as part of a polemical strategy. Admittedly, what has remained of modern autonomy exists only as the personal appropriation of powers that have long since been operative, but nothing human survives death if it is not inspired by a personal breath of renewal. Only a renewed, and thus modified, life can testify to the independence of original individuals. Thanks to the combination of individual uniqueness and tradition, philosophy shares a specific temporality with all parts of civilization and cultural history. A past cannot become the promise of a future if not for the alchemy of an original memory in the present.

The temporal schema of philosophizing that emerges here precedes the distinction between a speaker's addressing someone else and a reply that is expected from the listener. The concretization of this temporality can be found in the kind of "handing down" that we call "tradition." From a hermeneutical point of view, the history of philosophy is seen as the unfolding in different times of models according to which the present displaces itself as reinterpretation of an inheritance, which thereby has a future. However, such reinterpretation does not necessarily oppose the monological self-understanding of philosophy. If each thinker is an isolated retriever of what has been said before, the thinker's autonomy can be relativized by emphasizing the great extent to which each is nourished by the fables and systems of the tradition, but an understanding of philosophy that reduces it to a history of emerging and influential theories neglects the dialogical temporality of the speaking, writing, handing on and accepting, rejecting, or amending through which thinking philosophers propose to one another what they express of their reflective lives. The hermeneutical emphasis on the discourses that allegedly can be separated from the lives out of which they emerge, as if they were the product of anonymous powers, scarcely modifies the model of the traditional monologism. The history of effects [*Wirkungsgeschichte*] and the history of reception [*Rezeptionsgeschichte*] are important moments of philosophical developments, but the suggestion that the coherence of philosophy's history can be reduced to being nothing else than an integrative process would obscure or suppress its essential intersubjectivity. True, speaking, listening, and responding are impossible outside of all involvement in anonymous patterns and powers, but these would not be operative at all, if they were not handed down, tested, critically appropriated, discussed, and transformed by the worldwide community of philosophical interlocutors, who struggle not only with and in themselves but also with one another, while asking how they can make new sense of the various texts and traditions to which they refer.

Speaking and Listening: The Logic of Dialogue (Dialogic)

Addressing Saying exists only when a person speaks to another person. It is always an address that aims at someone directly. The person spoken to stands in the dative; he receives the address of the other. The speaker exposes herself in speaking by offering another something to understand. Her message is a double gift: (1) it offers a "said" (i.e., that which she says), and (2) it addresses a listener. By "saying" some said to the recipient, she invites a listener to reply to her said, i.e., to respond by giving or signifying something to the gift of the other. By reacting, the recipient in turn becomes a speaker and giver: his response exposes him to the first speaker and invites her to reply to him.

How is a speaker given to the listener? Not as an object that can be perceived as one of many objects. Still less as something useful that can be used. Neither does the speaker as speaker appear to the listener as one of the many members of the same community with whom the listener shares certain opinions, tasks, and habits.[6] For in all these modes of appearing, the speaker is perceived from the super- or meta-perspective of an outsider, not by the very listener who is involved in an address through which the speaker summons him to become an interlocutor. Addressing someone is not a mode of *being-with*; it is a targeting and facing and directing words or signs to another during the face-to-face of a confrontation. The phenomenon of being addressed is given to me only when I myself am the addressee and thus am invested by a new task: responding. The speaker is given to me, the listener, as a *you*, not as a *he* or *she* as part of a *we*. Insofar as addressing is essential to speaking, the speaker is always *you*.

As soon as the speaker is understood as mere participant of a surveyable totality, the address is lost. The latter mode of understanding is usual in the tradition of social philosophy. The philosopher then has adopted a perspective from which one can display the world as a social network in which human individuals are related to one another within the horizon of a whole. Surpassing the multiple perspectives of the various individuals insofar as these are caught in their interindividual perspectives and relations, one can then draw a panoramic overview, but the proper phenomenality of the facing and the face-to-face (addressing, speaking to, listening to, responding to, turning to, giving to) has then vanished. I, the philosopher, then observe the being-together and being-with-one-another of the many members of a social universe that can be characterized by its particular features. But if philosophy *itself* is a kind of addressing and speaking to others, no philosopher is able to raise himself to such a free-standing height above all those members (including himself) without immediately falling back into the interfacial discourse of someone who listens and talks to others about the surveys and overviews that resulted from that godlike superperspective. If speaking is always an address that provokes a response, philosophy cannot culminate in an egological overview, even if the ego in whose name the philosopher speaks is called "transcendental." When a philosopher, through solitary reflection, attempts to transcend the conversation in which he is entangled, he tries to surpass his strictly personal views as well as the particular views of his place and time in order to speak in the name of a completely unbiased and universal perspective (which no longer is a perspective): the perspective of a "transcendental" or (transcendent?) mind, ipseity, or "Ego." But how could he be successful in this enterprise without passing through innumerable confrontations with other standpoints, habits, views, and cultures? How can we escape the danger of reducing the ongoing history of philosophical conversations to a personal and particular—national, epochal, continental, or otherwise perspectival—view or a forever undecided competition between many different perspectives? In any case, neither isolation nor generalization can replace a multiplicity of dialogues.[7]

I and You Even a philosopher is either addressing or being addressed and is thus condemned to be a listener who responds. He cannot remove himself from the conversation, not even if his reflection demands that he be silent for a time. As a speaker, he is given, delivered over, to the person spoken to, a You for an I or an I for a You. As a person who speaks and writes, the philosopher certainly is a self with an initiative of his own, who speaks in the nominative. But at the same time, this self stands in the dative: without receiving many gifts from many speakers and writers, one can neither become nor be and remain a philosopher. Everyone who speaks returns a version of the words received.

Saying, with which everything human begins, reveals itself as a reciprocal event between you and me. It constitutes the horizon for all thinking (solitary as well as dialogical), but it loses its challenging character when it is reduced to an element within the unfolding of a synthesis produced by some overarching self. The ultimate horizon of philosophy is interpersonal, reciprocal, and temporal in sequences of addressing and replying. In this sense, philosophy is historical. The attempt to transcend this horizon by adopting a transcendental point of view, and thus to understand history as the unfolding of a transindividual power or principle, neglects the necessity of the Saying, without which that very point of view cannot faithfully express its own conviction.

Introduction to Philosophy We can approach the structure of the philosophical conversation by analyzing how one is initiated into philosophy. No one begins to philosophize by assuming the position of a solitary and autonomous ego over and against a totality of beings. Every participant begins by relying—at least to some extent—on the authority of one or more persons who are already at home in philosophy. To learn what philosophy is and how it is done, we went to teachers who guided us beyond the threshold that separates everyday opinions (*doxa*) and mores (*ethos*) from the domain of critical thought. The teacher urged us to reflect on current assumptions by selecting particular questions and texts, by leading us to individual thinkers, and by proposing certain paths to solutions or further questions. Later, we discovered that our teachers and the major thinkers to whom they appealed stood within certain traditions and handed down several assumptions that they did not fully prove. Every tradition of thought has also its own *doxa* and its own *ethos*, and we have in the meantime discovered that it is impossible to appropriate all that has been handed down to us by a plethora of thinkers. The beginning of any thinking is therefore not only authoritarian but also selective and particular. Even if we were capable of studying all the philosophical traditions and heroes of the past and present, it would still be impossible to evaluate them from without or from above, for every metahistorical and metaphilosophical point of view is itself a particular understanding of specific traditions. Any introduction to philosophy initiates students into a specific world in which the participants honor certain authors, opinions, styles, and fashions while forgetting or neglecting others. Particular individuals and schools fight for influence and power, but success among the majority, the general public, or the media is not guaranteed for the greatest thinkers nor for the most promising movements or the truth itself.

What students hear from their professors, their "said," they receive as a gift that must be accepted, at least in a hypothetical and provisional mode, although good professors will teach them also how, through much trial and error, they will become capable of making up their own proper mind. The students reply to their teachers by asking questions and inventing objections, and then by imitation of texts or teachers, which prepare them for their own, more personal forays into philosophy. Once they have become (co-)philosophizers, they are ready to become colleagues, capable of handing on or returning new versions of the gifts they have received. A discussion between mature philosophers has then become possible.

Discussion The asymmetry of the teacher/student relationship is retained in every dialogue. Saying something meaningful that is not trivial—even if it is only a question—qualifies someone as a teacher, but all teachers, even the greatest, have learned their wisdom from others. Participation in the philosophical community, thinking-with, is an interplay of suggestive provocation and critical acceptance as preparation for a reply, which, once received, invites a reply from the previous speaker or writer. When an authority speaks, I learn; when I respond, you might learn or not from me, but, in any case, you are challenged to a new response.

We assume here that the speaker has something interesting to say, something that gives the listener something to think about. It need not be completely new, for even what I already know can and does receive a new meaning in the mouth of another. The other's said need not be immediately perceived as interesting either, for perhaps I am not yet mature enough for the thought that is offered to me. The content's interest concerns what is said; the saying itself, however, is always new and surprising, because (a) it expresses the individuality of the speaker, and (b) it engages the addressee by requiring something of him or her. Addressing requires the production or reproduction of something said, which keeps the conversation going. It also contains a unique *demand*: apart from the content of the reply, it requires an appropriate mode of response. This is most clear in encounters during which hardly anything specific is said—in the case of a greeting, for example. Who knows what "Hello" means outside of the address in which the greeter exposes him- or herself? An extended hand or the tipping of a hat can replace the greeting, or one can smile at another or welcome her with a nod of the head; each time, the person greeted is confronted with an invitation and a demand. She is invited to "my" world, insofar as one offers her a place and a possibility of moving and acting in it, but at the same time, she is called upon to respond to my welcoming in an appropriate way. There are, however, cases in which the invitational aspect appears to be completely absent: the other person is not admitted at all into the space and time of the speaker. Such exclusion is similar to murder, because it dismisses the demand that is inherent to the other's emergence. It is a practical but also, at the same token, a theoretical denial of the other's appearance and existence. The Other's appearance as such is the first word and the first invitation, even if it happens silently.

Retrieving Emmanuel Levinas

At this point, I want to appeal to Emmanuel Levinas's phenomenology of the other. His works have shown how the Other's face awakens and addresses my conscience with a *moral* demand. The description of the other's facing or speaking *cannot* be limited to descriptive language; saying what and how the *fact* of the Other's emergence *is*—the mere "givenness" of the other (you) whom I happen to encounter—undeniably includes a confrontation with a normative, indeed moral, demand. Seeing you *is* discovering that I have a conscience; hearing your addressing me *is* awakening to the truth that I *must* respond to your presence in a way that is the contrary of being murderous. Your appearance commands me to become responsible for your life.

From a phenomenological perspective, the relation between the face's invitation, which demands a response, and my obligation to take responsibility for the other needs a precise description of the command that is implied in our encounter. I will not repeat here what I have written elsewhere on this question;[8] in the context of this chapter, I will instead restrict myself to a few, partly critical, remarks.

Asymmetry and Guilt Levinas describes the encounter with another person as the discovery of an essential inequality. Insofar as I spontaneously indulge myself in the pleasures of the world, your appearance awakens me to the awareness of your absolute and infinite "height" and, consequently, to a consciousness of myself as conscientious: obligated to and responsible for you. This relation is characterized by an essential asymmetry. To recognize this phenomenal "revelation" precedes and relativizes all speculative, phenomenological, and analytical approaches that take their departure from a dogmatically affirmed equality of all human subjects. Your existence reveals to me that the question of intersubjective equality and symmetry is secondary; in contrast to all attempts at deriving other "minds" from the self-consciousness of a (real or transcendental) ego, we must begin with the initial asymmetry that is given, when I (this real ego here and now *and always*) look at you as you, who look at me or speak to me. The accurate description of my (i.e., whatever real ego's) fundamental relation to you (i.e., whoever looks at me or speaks to me) does not imply that you experience me as "high" in the sense in which I experience your highness. However—and this is my first critical remark—it seems impossible to avoid discovering that—*from another perspective*—

you are *also* equal in dignity, rights, nature, rationality, etc., with all other human individuals, including me. This other perspective encompasses not only the traditional superperspective that displays all human individuals as instances of a human genus or universality but also Levinas's own perspective, which permits him to describe his own experience of the relation between you ("the" Other!) and me (every "me"!) in the form of a valid (phenomenological or transphenomenological) description that must be recognized as adequate by all his readers. If "the Other" ("you") *as such* is "high," and if I (as the one who, wherever and whenever, is confronted with the presence of an Other's existence) am the Other's servant, then the inequality expressed in this statement is as universally valid as there are persons in the situation of a facing You, related to a not only faced but also facing I. Levinas's descriptions of the asymmetry between you and me cannot be valid if they must not be affirmed by every ego who encounters another person. If Levinas is right, there is a *reciprocal but chiastic asymmetry between you and me. Reciprocity does not entail symmetry, and chiastic asymmetry includes mutuality.*[9]

Levinas perceives the absoluteness of the other (Kant would say, the other's dignity) not only as obligating but also as an *accusation.* I, whom you, as the other, look at or speak to, am a me (*un moi*) in the accusative: *me voici.* I am always already guilty, because I do not esteem you highly enough by not acting responsibly enough in favor of you. A guilty conscience in me is manifested by your appearance, because this appearance reveals my narcissistic complacency. I have never sufficiently fulfilled my most basic moral task and cannot ever hope to succeed perfectly in it.

However, there must be a moment in my awareness of you, in which I am not yet guilty: the awakening to the other is itself innocent, insofar as it reveals how I must respond to the other's appearance and how I will become guilty *if* my response is poor or inappropriate. That I do not give a completely correct response makes me guilty in some degree. It might be true that no one ever does or even can act fully appropriately, although it is difficult to know this, but in any case, there is a difference between the revelation of the demand that is given through the other's appearance and the discovery of my deficiency in replying adequately to this fact. I would like to suggest that this runs parallel with the difference between the dative and the accusative. When you, as the Other, address me, you place me in the dative. I receive your saying and what you say; you and your said are given to me as a gift to which I must react appropriately. The particular mode or manner in which I react to your invitation determines the extent to which I am good or bad. The accusation or the pardon that places me in the accusative comes later. If I can foresee egotistical features of my action, I can anticipate the accusation, but by itself the phrase *me voici* can just as well indicate a certain degree of willingness to service or hospitality.

The Beginning of Ethics What comes first is the gift of the word as the saying of a said, and the first reaction it invites is receptivity. If the gift is good, gratitude is appropriate. In saying a said, the giving presents not only a word, however; it also gives the giver. Self-giving deserves thanks, for even if someone approaches another with treacherous or murderous intentions, facing one's victim cannot entirely suppress the murderer's readiness to pay attention and get in touch. It is the contradiction between the meaning of their unwilled self-gift and the actual threat that gives murderers their outrageous cruelty.

The givenness of the other and the "dative" into which it puts me are constitutive for a basic law of ethics: because I cannot avoid responding to your gift, I am summoned to do this in an appropriate way, but there are ways of missing the mark. Your presence thus triggers my becoming either good or bad. Giving suggests receptivity and acceptance, thanks, welcoming, and hospitality, but these are not always easy. The worst rejection, murder, remains a temptation as long as the recipients' narcissism trumps humility. Judgment comes later; I should be accused if I fail to respond appropriately to your visitation, but our encounter as such cannot make me guilty. Openness to the gift awakens the possibility of my *becoming* good or bad, but it precedes all judging. Both receptivity and rejection are modes of affectivity: the appearance of another person affects me; dependent on the other's presentation and my own disposition, it elicits in me a particular attunement; by forbidding me to recoil into myself, it suggests care for the other, but I can make myself deaf or insensitive.

Ontology The second critical remark I would like to make with regard to Levinas's groundbreaking thought concerns his critique of ontology. You and I, as for-the-other, cannot be comprehended as two elements of a totality. If we understand "being" as the dynamic "essence" that connects all beings as moments of a network dominated by the exclusive interest of each moment in its own being, then neither you nor I can be called beings in any neutral sense at all. This is the reason why Levinas avoided ontological expressions as much as possible, when speaking about the Other and me and all other realities that—like you, me, death, time, hope, or love—he refused to call phenomena, because they cannot be ranged among the components of an—in his sense—"ontic" or "ontological" totality. "Revelation" and "epiphany" seemed to him more adequate expressions to name them in their radical difference from phenomenal manifestation and appearances. To approach them, we need a thinking beyond what he wants to call "ontology" and even beyond the dimension he later calls phenomenological.

Levinas's attempt to transcend being and phenomenality refers to a certain interpretation of Heidegger's thought of being (*Denken des Seins*), which Levinas saw as a summit of the European civilization. Because the Heideggerian framework cannot do justice to the emergence of the Other in its difference from being in the sense of "essence" and "inter-esse," Levinas concluded that the framework itself had to be broken. The Other is beyond the "essence": a "hole" in the world. In *Totalité et Infini,* Levinas still borrowed some terms from the ontological tradition to characterize that which surpasses being: "*kath'auto,*" "in itself," "absolute," infinite," etc. Later, however, he tried to radicalize this language by avoiding all ontological connotations, sometimes even by excluding the copula of the French he wrote, but in the end, he accepted that the thematizing character of philosophy excludes such radicalism.

In order to show that ontology, because of its thematizing character—even in its phenomenological versions—is not able to do justice to the dimension of the Other and therefore must point beyond its own horizon toward a beyond, Levinas introduced the distinction between "the said" and "the saying," which I have used in the preceding pages. Saying transcends the totality of all that can be thematized, gathered, said, because it has a fundamentally different structure, of which I have tried to indicate some features above. However, in writing or speaking about saying and its difference from the said, we inevitably treat it as a *topos* or theme, and this thematization betrays the saying's allegedly super- or nonthematic peculiarity.

Doesn't this mean that the saying disappears as soon as we think about it, because by doing so, we transmute it unavoidably into a said? Philosophical—and, in general, all thematic—approaches seem to conquer, recuperate, absorb, or destroy all attempts at escaping the thematization of Saying and the inexorable supremacy of the said. While speaking or writing about intersubjective relations and the revelations related to it, philosophy seems to do something that it is not capable of doing. *If* indeed philosophizing and thematizing are inseparable, it would pervert a most important phenomenon: the unique peculiarity of the saying and the giving, the receiving and the replying, on which it must rely to say anything at all.

If all speaking *about* any issue turns the issue into a theme of some saying, which itself cannot be captured in any said, and if philosophy only speaks *about* issues, philosophy necessarily misunderstands some of its most important topics, such as you and myself. The truth of these non-themes can then show itself only through supplemental corrections that incessantly try to strip away the thematizing character of the statements in which these non-themes have been caught. Such a philosophical correction is then attempted by "unsaying" the said (*dédire le dit*), but the attempt itself is again a form of thematization, which thus commits a new betrayal of the saying that should be performed. Only a straightforward "No" to the first perversion is valid. The correction has its validity only insofar as it negates the perversion of a saying that has passed into an unthematized and uncaptured past.

Consequently, this negation lacks its own positive truth, because it is a mere "*un*saying" without being capable of exhibiting its saying *within* philosophy.

If my encounter with you reveals a structure that explodes the horizon of all thematization, then, as long as we persist in speaking about things, we must choose between two possibilities: either (1) philosophy focuses only on things, objects, phenomena, and beings that fit the framework of thematizing discourses while excluding everything else from it; or (2) our reflection targets *all* that exists and shows—all "beings" and "phenomena"—including those that affect and strike and address, surprise, involve, overwhelm, and speak to us, even those realities that resist thematization, unsettling thereby our speaking about (but not to) it. In the first case, we restrict philosophy to only a *part*—and not the most interesting one—of all that captures our attention, whereas the second conception of philosophy must invent a more appropriate language in order to remain loyal to those phenomena that can only be *faced*, received, responded to, or thanked for but not objectified, displayed, or thematized.

So long as we talk *about* the Other, we cannot avoid that the Other's epiphany, precisely by virtue of its radical difference from all thematizable beings, be ranged among and compared to them. But does philosophy have perspectives, concepts, or words to clarify The Other's nonthematic peculiarity? *If* "being" were accepted as only a name for all that permits thematization, would we then be completely unable to distinguish the meaning of a radically "other than being" (*autrement qu'être*)? If so, how could we even mention it?

If we opt for the second possibility by insisting on the true universality of being and the philosophical ultimacy of ontology, we must give up the monopoly of thematizing thought within the horizons of philosophy. Life itself, however, bridges the tear between the epiphany of the Other *to whom* we speak and the appearance of other phenomena *about which* we can speak. A philosophy that does not forget or betray life must therefore realize the unity of its saying and its said in each of its allocutions. If thematizing cannot grasp this unity as such, the reason for it lies in the intentionality of thematization itself.

Only if "being" and phenomenality as such were unthinkable without focusing on their thematizable aspects, only then would an ontology of intersubjectivity be essentially unfit to honor you and our relationship by celebrating in thought how amazing you and we *are*. Should we not recognize that your and my existence are too important to let philosophy exclude us from its orbit, even if we must accept a certain distance between the life we live and our philosophical insufficiency in capturing the double dative we perform while speaking and listening in our sequences of challenge and response?

Within philosophy, most saying or writing is thematizing. It is then philosophizing itself that objectifies the phenomena in themes and theses. That the being of personal and intersubjective phenomena cannot fully manifest itself is a consequence of the specific kind of speaking that is cultivated in Western philosophy. Philosophers have always known that certain wonders are incomprehensible, even for them. Philosophical theology is in this respect the classical example of a thinking that has repeatedly criticized and destroyed its own thematizing in order to free its own said from its unavoidable and unconquerable limitations. Now that we are beginning to reflect on the ontological status of intersubjective phenomena, we discover that these likewise are too mysterious and too incomprehensible for philosophical consideration, at least within the style that currently holds sway.

As phenomenology, philosophy must uncover the differences between the various kinds of phenomenality, but as the source of thematizing discourses, it makes everything homogeneous. As long and insofar as philosophy speaks about *ta panta* and *to pan* without clarifying its speaking as such, it remains confined to writing treatises about thematizable phenomena. Other phenomena, such as the communication between philosophers, without which philosophy cannot exist, are then practiced but not opened up within philosophy.

Addressing Thought Yet it is possible to acknowledge the uniqueness of the other person *in language*—and even in philosophical discourse. Not in a mere speaking *about* speaking and speakers as speakers, but instead by addressing someone as you, i.e., not as a particular instance of human being and other in general but as you yourself: you alone and unique. By directing my words to you, I reach you, not merely as an instance or individualization of "the other," but you as this unique you here and now or there and then, who is neither me, nor another incarnation of "the I," nor an example of you-in-general. Insofar as you are addressed by me, you cannot be thematized, but you can be spoken to without reducing you to a theme or *topos*.

You likewise are a speaker who listens and replies; i.e., you too address me who addresses you. Being involved in this conversation, neither you nor I are master of the dialogue that unfolds between you (no other than this unique you) and me (not any other me). Our being caught in the sequence of a mutually summoning speech cannot be described as some instantiation of a universal concept like "conversation" or "dialogue." The challenges through which you and I force each other to focus on a common question or phenomenon set the stage for our exchange. They force us to think along lines that neither you nor I can monopolize. Our thoughts and speeches are stimulated, but neither you nor I can summarize the unfolding dialogue as a unified said that belongs to you or me alone. The meaning of "I think" is in this context certainly very different from the Cartesian Cogito, which for several centuries has symbolized the arrogance of a master philosopher who believes in the possibility of a solitary autonomy.

The allocutionary structure of authentic dialogues complicates the standard method of philosophy. Insofar as thinking includes a personal address, because it cannot exist without being addressed and answered, the relations between singular thinkers are *constitutive* for their *sayings* and, consequently, for their saids. What they tell or propose to one another would hover over the human condition without ever interesting anyone, if it were not anchored in the manifold of unique you's and I's that challenge one another by their proposals and counterproposals.

The only way philosophy can do justice to the intersubjectivity that is constitutive of its essence lies in the to and fro of the mutual addressing and responding through which unique persons seek a partly shared and partly different understanding that does not abolish entirely their own unique perspectives but rather creates a community of thought, even if a final unison cannot be formulated. Instead of meditating monologically as lonely egos-in-the-world who dispatch their messages in the form of anonymous generalities, philosophers must recognize that they are always already involved in the warp and woof of ongoing dia- or polylogues. By offering something said or written, they reveal themselves while affecting interlocutors. Not only the adequacy of what is said but also the fittingness of their inter- and allocutive behavior belongs to their task. Correctness of the communicative gesture itself has more to do with virtue than with logic, but logic must be recognized as one minimal condition of their communication. Further analysis would introduce an ethics of philosophizing: the gift of speaking and the correct ways of replying demand their own appropriate behavior. Gratitude, respect, reverence, courage, and generosity are required, and many ways of violating the required *dia-logic* are possible.

I am aware that my plea for recognition of your and my and everyone's unicity has again—and perhaps inevitably—fallen into a series of generalizations. But the point remains that everyone who writes or speaks is caught in a saying that cannot be replaced by any said. That you are you and I am I without being reducible to being mere instances of some anonymous generality is recognized by life, without a doubt. It remains true *within* philosophy, if we do not want to suppress or ignore a primary condition of its possibility.

TWO

On the Unity of Thematic Philosophy and the History of Thought

Some decades ago, the very complete bibliographic *Repertorium* of the *Revue Philosophique de Louvain* listed more than two-thirds of all recent publications in philosophy as dedicated to historical subjects and less than one-third to thematic ones. The proportions might have changed, but the production of studies in the history of philosophy is still abundant, especially in "continental" philosophy. There are, however, many among the faculty who think that the history of thought has little to do with the task of an authentic philosopher. They restrict the past of philosophy to a mere preparation that—like the past of physics or biology—is overcome by today's thematic philosophy. According to them, the study of the past is not necessary for solving our philosophical problems, and the best introduction consists in a presentation of the ongoing debates about actual topics.

The defenders of this position will have to indicate a borderline between the history of philosophy and the actuality of contemporary philosophy, but they rarely thematize this difficult question as such. The philosophical present they recommend does not consist in a timeless here and now but rather in a recent—and thus already bygone—

constellation of philosophical problems, currents, and developments, i.e., in a *recent past* of philosophy. But how can we draw a clear-cut and philosophically justified distinction between our recent past and the extended past of history? Not only does this distinction seem to be a rather vague one, but a more fundamental question about separating philosophy's actuality from its history asks why a more *recent past* of philosophy would or should be more relevant for our philosophizing than a *more remote* philosophical past, which includes many more classics than the recent history of philosophy.

Some might respond to these questions by asking rhetorically: Hasn't the great progress in science and technology, during the last centuries, given convincing proof of progress? Doesn't this exemplary progress give us enough reasons and means to distinguish our present epoch from earlier ages of experience and thought? Such a response assumes that the modern faith in progress on all fronts of theory, including philosophy, is justified. Against that faith, I will defend here that progress in philosophy cannot be compared to the progress of natural sciences and that a similar faith in philosophical progress, as if it had obtained triumph after triumph during the last centuries, has already been refuted by the many contrasts and hostilities that today divide a great number of singular philosophers and philosophical schools. But let us begin with the question of whether human individuals are able to philosophize without being supported by the experiences that their predecessors have had with it.

If total independence from the past is not possible in philosophy, must we then conclude that even the most original and creative philosopher is conditioned by written or spoken products that are already there, for example, in the form of a tradition or school in which one has been initiated? Similar questions can be asked about art, religion, morals, language, and all other dimensions of human culture. The answer seems to be in all cases that we never originate anything completely new but always take over, repeat, and—at least to some extent—transform the linguistic, moral, religious, artistic, philosophical patterns and traditions that have been produced before we arrived on the scene. All the discontinuities of human history cannot undo the fact that no human performance is entirely original. A human product is always, at least partially, the reproduction or supersession of something old: the renewal of a past that is accepted in a particular or individual—and to this extent also new and original—way. Human speech, prayer, art, and philosophy are re-creations of exemplary speeches, prayers, works of art, and philosophies that have come to us from a stretch of history that has already passed, whether that history is near or far from us in time. The most original (re)creations renew certain classics or traditions by a less predictable or expected sort of continuation; they transform a part of history whose first sources have disappeared into an unknown or mythical prehistory. Human creativity is—especially in hindsight—an only partly predictable transformation of an undeniable facticity on the basis of its acceptance. If all "original" philosophy relies on philosophical attempts that have been undertaken before it emerges, a certain past is an essential constituent of it. Philosophical activity is therefore not described adequately as the present production of a true insight into reality; the description must also include the dependence of the relatively new thinking on the facticity of thoughts produced before the actual thinkers—as heirs of a newly appreciated legacy—encounter them.

With regard to the future, we see a similar but mirrored relation: the lessons and texts in which a philosopher's thought is expressed are meant to be heard or read, understood and thought anew by others who, in their different times, prolong, redevelop, and change their heritage. The actuality of philosophy is the *present* but already *passing* transformation of an at once received, selected, and evaluated *past* into a not quite predictable *future*. Philosophers reproduce problems and solutions that are neither altogether new nor wholly identical with those of their predecessors, but their own texts are again invitations to a diversity of retrievals in the form of new meditations and results.

The temporal structure of philosophical thought, which thus comes to the fore, rules not only the relations that connect each philosopher to certain predecessors and traditions (which are not always the same) but also the philosophizing of each individual taken in isolation. If a philosophical work is the unfolding of a coherent thought, it cannot exist as a static whole, because no human individual is capable of realizing such a totality at once. A vast system like Hegel's *Encyclopedia,* Aquinas's *Summa,* or Spinoza's *Ethics* is never the all-embracing thought of one single day or hour. By concentrating on a combination of one encompassing concept—for example, *Esse, Substance,* or *Spirit*—with its unfolding in subordinate levels, divisions, and subdivisions, we can gather a coherent number of constituent parts into a synthesis, but we cannot have at the same time a clear and distinct idea of all its elements and all the relations that connect them to one another and to the whole. An insightful concept of some systematic totality presupposes that one rethink, in successive phases of time, the descriptions, analyses, argumentations, and subordinate connections thanks to which, by way of an all-encompassing résumé, that whole was progressively composed. We are incapable of thinking at once of such a complicated superconcept, including the time-consuming movements back and forth involved in it. Most often, our representation of a philosophical system consists in a global idea supported by a rather vague memory of the steps and stages that were developed by the producer during the process of its genesis.[1] The concept of a systematic totality presupposes a sort of historical *anamnesis* and the possibility of a certain *confidence.* Since it is impossible to check continually the solidity of past descriptions, analyses, and proofs, every philosopher has to rely on a certain trust: once we have checked the foundations, laid and relaid down before us, we confide that they are stable enough to support the further considerations on which we are focused here and now.

The discursivity of human thought imposes a temporal structure on the *cogitation* of every *Ego.* Even from a monological (or "egological") perspective, systematic reflection constantly depends on former reflections, the results of which constitute a personal past. This past must be remembered and trusted if the philosopher wants to make progress. But memory and trust are not enough. By memorizing the thoughts that have emerged until this point of life, a philosopher gathers a personal past. But philosophy is more than *anamnesis;* it is also a restless *renewal* of the partial truth that has been reached before. Even a solipsistic philosophy cannot exist except in the form of a personal microhistory. No systematic philosophy can escape the universal law of temporality. Even a philosophical monologue is the active production, correction, or retrieval of a philosophical history, and even a very egocentric philosopher remains in dialogue with philosophical reflections of the past.

If the history of philosophy, rather than being a museum or parade of frozen systems, is a series of transformations, then the historical character of all philosophy is obvious. No philosophy has started from itself, and all philosophers have begun as pupils. They were introduced to philosophy by teachers and texts that referred to other texts and teachers, and so forth. Nobody becomes a philosopher unless he or she is, as Diotima would say, "generated in the beauty" of a philosophical life.[2] The first philosophical knowledge of new philosophers consists in the repetition of lessons received from teachers who started their philosophical life before them and from a textual heritage that attracts those who will use it in a fecund way. Students of philosophy become adult by conquering a distance toward the fathers and mothers who educated them by urging them to appropriate critically elements of their thought. However, never can they altogether cut the umbilical cords attaching them to thinkers and traditions of the past. By combining and developing the structures of *generation, education, learning, criticism,* and *self-conscious thinking,* presupposed by all thematic philosophy, we can draw a picture of philosophical life as a differentiated genealogy of one or more families of thinkers. The story of all thinking families constitutes the history of philosophy. It contains more than an epic of philosophical relationships between singular individuals. A complete treatment of philosophical life would not only describe, analyze, and understand the existing relations between various individuals and families within one overall realm of philosophy but also connect them with a host of prephilosophical opinions, tastes, orientations, perspectives, and with the social, economic, political, aesthetic, and religious facts and structures of their contexts. A complete diagnosis of the world in which a certain philosophy originated will certainly help us to understand its problems, methods, and answers, but some productive philosophers will be more interested in the question of what they can learn from other philosophies than in the "merely" historical question of how the philosophical variety of each epoch coheres or contrasts with its social, political, artistic, and religious patterns and tendencies.

The difference between the perspective of a thematic philosopher and the perspective of a historian generates a difference between two sorts of philosophical history. Whereas the typically philosophical way of writing philosophy's history emphasizes conceptual and systematic connections, the historian's history of philosophy is a complex interdisciplinary study that has hardly been developed. But in both cases, the actuality of philosophy cannot be understood without a reconstruction of the past.

Because professional philosophers cannot perform their work if they ignore what others have discovered before them, the most self-aware among them have a penchant for intraphilosophical genealogies. Insofar as they are primarily interested in their predecessors' originality and the philosophical tradition they want to renew, their account of the past will highlight the theoretically inventive and innovative intentions of past thinkers and the philosophical possibilities they detect in the transmitted heritage. Most often, therefore, their histories present a sequence of texts that follow from former texts according to a temporal and more or less logical pattern of succession. If historians of philosophy lose or entirely bracket their interest in the truth, they may try to observe the philosophies of yesterday and today from a philosophically disengaged standpoint. They might be interested in other aspects of the history than those that fascinate philosophers, for example, in the social effects of various systems.

In this chapter, I concentrate on the standard history of philosophy as practiced by philosophers and its relation to the actual practice of today's philosophers in their own right. The question of the historically justified character of that standard must be left for a discussion with professional historians.

In the preceding pages, I stated that the activity called "philosophy" is not a creation *ex nihilo* but rather a new and differently productive reproduction of philosophical thoughts written and pronounced in the past. Every philosophy is a transformative continuation of one or more preceding philosophies or parts of them. All philosophers start as readers or listeners, learning what other philosophers already have discovered. Because there are only a few really great philosophers, most philosophers focus on retrieval and further unfolding of the philosophical tradition by writing or teaching notes or commentaries on the classics. This fact has consequences for the study of philosophy. A first-year student listens to a teacher who is supposed to be at home in philosophy. The teacher, however, presents and interprets the thoughts of one or more creative philosophers, most of whom are dead. The borderline between interpretation and creation is, however, difficult to draw, because even the most creative philosopher constantly refers—explicitly or implicitly—to texts and sayings of the past. Moreover, every philosopher is, as Husserl put it, an "eternal beginner," and all creations thrive on the interpretation of past philosophies.

Yet creative philosophy presupposes that one has become independent and "autonomous" in thinking. The interpretive or hermeneutic aspect of (re-)creative philosophy certainly contains elements of newness that cause ruptures and discontinuities. The passage from explanation to creation or from dependence to philosophical originality traverses a negative and positive critique of the philosophy received while listening and reading. By testing the texts of exemplary philosophers, the students find their own ways of becoming philosophers in their own right: unique individuals who hunt the truth at their own risk and responsibility. Strong but sensible criticism brought forward by passionate pupils is part of our progress in thought. The historical activity called "philosophy" aims at a creative reproduction through which admired thoughts are transmitted while being submitted to correction, reordering, and transformation into better approaches to the truth. *All* philosophical production is therefore both gratefully indebted to tradition and hopefully reaching out onto an uncertain future. But even mediocre teachers add a twist of their own to the philosophies they transmit.

The temporality of all systematic philosophy confronts the thinking subject with the *otherness* of a factual past, which he cannot change but only retrieve, and with a possible future that he cannot handle as he likes, although he contributes to it through texts, which—if read—might be retrieved by independent others. The otherness of time cannot be abolished by the present of a philosophical synthesis that encompasses all pasts in a vision *sub specie aeternitatis*. If such a vision were possible, it would constitute a perennial System in which the complete truth would be expressed once and for all. No other change or novelty would be possible in philosophy than the translation of this system into different languages of different spaces and times. The System would be equal to the Truth, and the history of philosophy would consist in a progressive unfolding and application of this truth. The last philosopher could then tell how the true system has developed itself from prephilosophic elements, through various discoveries, adventures, conflicts, and battles, into the completeness it has reached in the end.

This is the Hegelian conception of the relationship between systematic philosophy and its history. Just as religion in Hegel's conception is the truth insofar as it manifests itself in the form of feelings, images, and stories, the history of philosophy is an imperfect way of telling the truth: a conceptual narrative that presents the articulation of the system as a temporal succession of stages along the journey of exploration. Religion is imperfect because it does not transcend the level of representation (*Vorstellung*)—a level that still involves some distance between the knowing mind and the known. The story of philosophy, however, is a story about concepts, or rather about the total Idea, as it manifests itself progressively in successive configurations of a conceptual nature. The Idea is the supreme level where being and thought (or the ideal) have become identical. As successive in time, however, the history of philosophy is still imperfect, because it tells the story of the Idea's unfolding as a temporal adventure and not in its most authentic form: as the conceptual self-revelation of the timeless Absolute, in which all times are *aufgehoben* because they are only partial and relative expressions of the truth.

Although the past and the future of systematic philosophy are inextricably linked to its present stage, they maintain the irreducible otherness of their nonpresence to the present. This is a strong argument against the Hegelian conception according to which the history of philosophy is a reflection of the true system in the mirror of time. There is, however, a stronger and more radical form of *otherness*, which is also a condition of the possibility for both the history of philosophy and the unfolding of a systematic philosophy. It is the otherness of *other philosophers*.

In order to conquer independence in the realm of thought, a beginning philosopher must engage in a trial of strength with one or more others who have already achieved important works. A first condition for this conquest is the encounter with a good teacher who knows where to find the great philosophers and how to meet them through reading and interpretation of their texts. A second condition is that the teacher and the texts do not seduce the student to stop at agreement but provoke him to take responsibility for a thinking of his own. Sheer identification with a ready thought produces epigonism, whereas merely negative criticisms hardly produce anything. The exploitation of a philosophical heritage, however, presupposes emancipation.

Philosophical children try to overcome their dependence by destroying whatever ties them to longstanding traditions. Nothing seems to be true to some of them if it is not the most original expression of one's most subjective and concrete experience. No emancipation seems possible without contradiction, and thus, no emancipation without "fathers" or "mothers" who evoke resistance in their students. Their best service to the latter is perhaps the strength with which they not only sustain but also provoke and demand intelligent critique in response to their lessons.

By extending the indicated schema to the whole of philosophical history, we can show that the genealogy of philosophy is structured no less by polemical than by familial relationships. The picture of a philosophical history that results from this schema differs greatly from the Hegelian and the scientific picture of one gradual but continuous progress toward the only true and total truth. The relative independence of individual philosophers contradicts the idea of a completely true knowledge, of which individual philosophies would only be preparatory stages or partial links. The real truth of philosophy and its history is that of a plurality of thinkers who owe to others more than they can tell. While transforming everything, they receive it into their (partly borrowed) property, they can become repetitious epigones or uncommitted storytellers, but a more promising result of their highly useful work lies in the justification of transformative revivals that become again parts of philosophy's history.

The idea of appropriating what others have discovered ceases to be repulsive as soon as we notice that the resulting philosophy, if it is indeed a worthwhile transformation, includes a great deal of generosity. The emergence of an original thought is its revelation to others, who may appropriate and integrate it into their conceptual property, if they want and are able to hand it on as their own. Collective philosophies are epigonisms and therefore moribund or already dead, but no thinker repeats another's philosophy without changing it at least to some degree. If some philosophers happen to have the same thoughts as their originator, they might be good interpreters—but would they count in the history of thought? The story of philosophy is not a collective repetition of one or more philosophies but instead a lively history of irreducible differences, discussions, and polemics without end, held together by a basic congeniality of the participants.

If philosophy is an ongoing debate among living and dead individuals, *dialogue* is its dominant structure. No explanation of any philosophy will be adequate unless it shows how its author responds to problems and answers given by other philosophers and how the new philosophy has revealed new, not yet discovered or forgotten, possibilities. If philosophy is a dialogue, it is impossible to distinguish its thematic from its historical past and the future it opens up by each time updating or reenlivening it.

I seem, however, during the preceding argument, to have forgotten the important distinction between a *recent past* of today's philosophical discussions and the *remote past* of the exemplary Ancients. Aren't we more at home in the philosophical context of the last decades than in sixteenth-century, medieval, or Greek philosophy? Accurate understanding of old texts demands great efforts and a complicated, sometimes even painful, journey into the past. Even the temporal continuity of Western philosophy does not abolish the estrangement we experience when we try to familiarize ourselves with the thoughts of other epochs.

Yet it is not quite true that all those who live today are more familiar with the most recent productions of our culture—and, among them, with contemporary philosophy—than with old philosophies. Often the contrary is the case. For instance, not many philosophers really know the latest developments. Sensational and faddish changes might have some impact, but most of them die soon, whereas the most radical renovations can remain hidden, strange, or widely resisted for ages. The philosophy of Heidegger, for example, needed a long time before it was accepted by more than a happy few as a crucial event that changed the course of philosophy. Most often, we need ample time to discover the promises that are contained in the most recent thought. In philosophy, the general taste, as found in average textbooks, can stick to philosophical styles that were developed fifty, one hundred, or even two hundred years ago. Eighteenth-century Enlightenment, (neo-)Kantian, (neo-)Hegelian, and (neo-)positivist presuppositions still determine large parts of our context, many actual discussions are framed by methodical assumptions of old philosophies, and utilitarianism stubbornly hangs onto its popularity.

A more or less clear distinction between the remote and the recent past could perhaps be accommodated by extending the notion of "our recent past" to the entire epoch of modern philosophy. Thematic philosophy could then be delimited by the contemporaneity of those philosophers who—from Hobbes and Descartes to our days—are still invoked as participants in today's discussions. Such a division might be welcomed by those who like to make a distinction between the *thematic* relevance of former philosophies, insofar as today's discussions still refer to them, and the *historical* reality of what their authors have actually said and written. To the extent that the latter is no longer relevant for our own century, it would then have no other than a merely archeological interest.

However, can the distinction between thematic relevance and historical interest legitimate a separation between philosophy and its history? Not if we are unable to make a clear distinction between the philosophically living and the philosophically dead, i.e., between thoughts (or promises of thought) that contain truth or are close to it and thoughts that have lost their power to guide, challenge, or stimulate our reflection. But how can we establish such a distinction? By no other means than by actual thinking in our own name. Only by rethinking seemingly dead texts can we give them a chance to deliver their approaches to the truth. *All* texts are dead and mute as long as they are not resuscitated by a new rethinking here and now, thanks to which they speak again, albeit through voices other than the original ones. Besides, in order to become critical toward ourselves and to overcome our own illegitimate assumptions—for example, the assumption that we already know which elements of older texts are promising and which are not—we need to meet certain "strangers" who come from afar or from other times. Wasn't that, for example, one of the reasons why Socrates had to listen to the visitors from Elea?

The distinction between the modernity of "our time" and the prehistory of modern times should not be abolished. The Greek, the Roman, the various cultures of the Middle Ages are so different from our culture that we cannot quote most of their texts as documents that every interlocutor is familiar with. Heraclitus, Epicurus, Scotus are "others" and "strangers" in a more obvious and deeper sense than Locke, Newton, Kant, and Marx. But our greater distance from the former might contain more surprising promises for courageous travelers who succeed in breaking open their treasure chests. The difference between modern and premodern philosophers should, however, not be exaggerated, because spiritual kinship is not a simple question of chronology. One need not be ashamed for feeling closer to Plato or Aquinas than to Marx or Quine, and modernism is not necessarily a sign of being up to date. It remains, however, a fact that philosophers of older times with whom we feel familiar have expressed their thoughts in languages and contexts that demand cautious and slow deciphering before we can hear and rethink their explanations.

A fair understanding of a philosophy that is not our own demands that we sufficiently distance ourselves from our own convictions and insights, in order to approach the impersonality of a methodic tabula rasa in which the other philosophy can imprint its own particularity. This device is not only valid for the study of ancient or medieval philosophies but also for contemporary thoughts. Moreover, the differences among works of our own century can be more radical than the differences that separate certain works of different ages. True, with contemporary philosophers we share more similarities of language, science, politics, ways of life, morality, information, and so on, but in other respects, for instance on the level of religion and philosophy, no one should feel ashamed about feeling a deeper affinity with Plato, St. Augustine, or Spinoza than with Sartre or Derrida.

The strangeness of other philosophies is an analogous concept that must be clarified with the help of distinctions regarding the individuality of the various philosophers; the originality of their style; their mode of participation in discussions of their epoch; their belonging to philosophical schools, groups, or tendencies; their dependence on particular contexts; and their figuring in constellations of affinity and hostility. The concrete realization of all these aspects would draw a variegated map of philosophy in different periods of civilization. Within such a period, a philosophy will appear as more or less exceptional or strange according to its greater or lesser originality (which is not equivalent with truth). Absolute strangeness appears when we cannot find any way of access that permits us to rethink the texts we try to decipher. If these remain a closed book, we cannot tell whether they contain worthwhile thoughts or not. Another limit of strangeness, a sort of zero value of otherness, is reached when a philosophy is so obvious that it deprives us of every distance. A promising acquaintance with other philosophers is only possible between the limits of absolute otherness and straightforward or putative triviality. A certain degree of difference seems essential for the possibility of learning from others. If we are too familiar with a philosophy, for example, if it does not contain anything other than the conceptual unfolding of what we recklessly call "common sense," we cannot learn from it, except, perhaps, a sort of disgust caused by endless rumination. In philosophy, too, the only way to be saved from obsessive narcissism lies in a hard struggle with authentic otherness. A good deal of positivistic reconstruction is necessary if we want to escape from the inbreeding caused by endless monologues that kill all inspiration. This need for a challenging alienation does not contradict the primacy of systematic philosophy; it is an essential moment of it. Positivism and hermeneutics together generate the philosophical kinship thanks to which every philosophy depends on former philosophies, being at the same time an original appropriation and a transformative revolution.

The Greco-European history of philosophy is a long series of attempts to reduce the originality and otherness of former philosophies by (re-)creative revitalization. Quite a number of such attempts are presented as fragments, moments, variations, or preparatory stages of one overall, final, and triumphant philosophy. One of the most naïve ways of explaining the many differences between the historical philosophies is expressed in the conception of their history as an ongoing discovery of true theories, which is at the same time a progressive elimination of false theses and demonstrations. According to this conception, the task of a systematic philosopher does not include any historical knowledge, although it may sometimes be useful to know how a good argument came into existence or was corrected and reformulated by a particular author.

Another view rejects the presupposition that the main philosophical problems remain unchanged while the methods and answers change. It sees that the story of philosophy includes a story of its changing problematic. The questions asked by philosophers change with the historical experiences of individual and collective lives within particular societies and cultures. The understanding and formulation of the questions from which each serious philosophy starts, the perspective of the search, and the ways one tries to approximate the truth are integral parts of its central question and of the task to be accomplished. None of the questions asked can be taken over uncritically, for every start and every step must be justified within philosophy itself. Consequently, the history of philosophy includes a history of the questions that are asked and of the reasons why these questions—and no others—are asked in the way in which they are.

Hegel, who saw this point, believed that it was possible to interpret not only the answers of former philosophies but also their questions as elements of different totalities or "figures of the mind," figures that themselves were (a) partial anticipations and (b) subordinate elements of one final totality: the encompassing truth of the perfect system.

After Hegel, the only way of simultaneously affirming the *particularity* of all past philosophies *and* the essential *universality* of the unique and total truth seems to consist in the postulate that all specimens of authentic, serious, and radical thought *must* converge somehow in one overall truth ("the whole that is the truth"), which transcends and *needs* their particularities. Notwithstanding *and because of those particularities,* all serious philosophies are partial expressions of the one and unique truth. However, Hegel does not explain how the final philosophy can be found in a last, non-, or supraparticular system. According to his logic, that system would tie all truth-loving philosophers together into one spiritual family of thinkers who think the same truth—but who exactly would be responsible for presenting it? Would all of these thinkers share one common consciousness or idea? Would their singularities, with all their existentially and philosophically relevant differences, no longer matter, or would these differences be so superficial that one could neglect them? Is any human capable of fathoming the ultimate union in truth that, we hope, will crown the plurality of our attempts at approaching it? The diversity of these attempts and our (always provisional) results do not necessarily hurt our tentative communion. But even if we postulate that our ways and those of our predecessors and successors will come together, such a convergence might not take the form of a final system. It seems more cautious—and, hopefully, closer to the truth—to understand the history of philosophy as an endless discussion that keeps philosophers apart and together in mutual proposals and counterproposals or—more modestly—in (re-)creative proposals that make the past fecund for a truth-loving future.

THREE

The Relevance of Intersubjectivity for First Philosophy and the History of Philosophy

"FIRST PHILOSOPHY"?

If all attempts to reach an altogether pure, free, or transcendental viewpoint in philosophy are condemned to fail, the idea of a discipline called "first philosophy" also seems to be indefensible.[1] The transcendental Ego so ardently sought, the search itself, perhaps even all attempts at methodological and metaphilosophical foundation are then no more than fragments of a global process that characterized a particular period of history. The authors of these fragments could not free themselves from their dependence on certain hidden roots, in order to lay these roots and perhaps other relevant conditions of their thought bare. However, philosophy has become aware of having long ago embarked upon a collective and personal history whose exact genealogy has disappeared behind the horizon of its discoveries. Thinkers find themselves caught in situations where so much has already been decided that their thought appears to be the product of borrowings they do not fully possess rather than being a creation ex nihilo of their own originality. Often, their subjectivity seems to be an effect or symptom of a powerful thought and language that speaks through them. The patterns, individual metaphors, and literary traditions of their time and place capture them without permitting them an escape.

The Hegelian conviction that we can master and integrate the history of our thoughts by means of an insight into the rational reconstruction of their necessary unfolding has lost its spell. Aren't we too profoundly convinced of the contingencies and absurdities of history? Are we still able to reconcile ourselves, through a rational reconstruction, with a philosophical drama in which our own role is as inevitable as it is alienated, because it surpasses our power to freely think and write what we most properly feel or think or want?

If we lack sufficient distance from our own involvement in the ongoing history of philosophy to map out the departures, routes, and arrivals of the journey on which we have embarked, we must recognize that we are caught in a labyrinth whose layout remains unknown. Can we, in this situation, still uphold the project of a "first philosophy"? Does this expression not imply the possibility of isolating the fundamentals of philosophy, which should be determined before the other parts can be built upon a secure basis established once and for all? Does the assumption of this possibility not imply a particular conception of philosophy, in which basis, ground, point of departure, blueprint, method, construction, hierarchy, and so on play the leading roles? Is the enterprise of a "first philosophy" necessarily connected to the idea that, first, we must secure an ultimate "foundation" before we can do anything worthwhile in philosophy? And does this idea condemn all of us to the fate of "eternal beginners," which has dominated philosophical history from Descartes to Husserl?

However, if we are to abandon completely any search for some kind of absolute to which everything else refers, it seems that the very idea of truth equally must be renounced. Aren't we then building on quicksand or just playing and dancing around? If, on the contrary, practicing philosophy still is tied to the possibility of a certain approximation to the truth, an ultimate and all-encompassing horizon seems to remain the ineluctable noema of a most radical noësis, which is at once a passion and the very core of thinking. If we abandon the intention of all intentions in philosophy, what could then protect us against a mere relativism of equally disappointing perspectives? How would it be possible to love the truth in a nonsuperficial way, if we cannot even maintain the *idea* of our universe as a meaningful and at least somewhat orderly constellation—as well as the *idea* of a subject able to think in a universally recognizable and valid way?

If serious thought is to remain possible, the *idea* of truth must be maintained and loved as an absolute and all-encompassing idea that cannot be discarded. Against the sensationalism of total contingency, the idea of truth has at least the *regulative* value of maintaining a distinction between *more* and *less* adequate proposals, a distinction without which no approach of truth, progress, hope, or passion in philosophy would be possible. A certain form of relativism seems inevitable, but a wholly uncompromising—and thus absolute and nonrelative—relativism excludes the possibility of any judgment about the value of a particular philosophy. The only other possibility seems to lie in a purely formal or aesthetic evaluation of philosophical productions. If the "content" of all theories becomes indifferent with regard to truth, we can only appreciate the elegance, the originality, or the beauty of their presentation.

The emotional intensity of philosophical utterances—and, as we will see, their style—is not completely alien to the question of their truth. For, even if it were not possible to check their truth or falsehood by purely conceptual means, we would still have an affective experience of their being warm or cold, exciting or boring, interesting or trivial, profound or frivolous, sensational or serious, and so on. The degree of philosophical proximity to truth corresponds to kinds of feeling and intuition or recognition, in which our desire for truth shows itself to be perhaps the only remaining power in our labyrinth. However, the question of whether truth is the most adequate name for the most desirable goal of philosophy cannot be answered immediately. Has it perhaps more to do with an ideal form of fecundity?[2]

HERMENEUTICS AND THE ANONYMOUS

The evolution of phenomenology has convinced many philosophers that the struggle for capturing the truth within the boundaries of a universally valid system—notwithstanding its metaphilosophical and metamethodological refinements and emendations—has not prepared the terrain for a radical revolution comparable to the revolutions of Parmenides, Plato, Descartes, or Kant but rather for a variety of hermeneutic renewals of the factual situation into which they are raised. On the basis of the three millennia traversed by the historical praxis of philosophy, with which one can become familiar through reading, we should gratefully appropriate, integrate, and thus thoroughly transform this great heritage into our own versions of it. Our situation involves us in a critical and partially renovating form of agreement with inherited opinions and stories, a specific language, a historical and biographical past, particular patterns of obviousness, ethos, behavior, and so on. All our reflection has been preceded and is supported by a naïve participation in a particular community and history of speech, imagination, evaluation, opinion, and practice. The sharing of a specific culture permeates all reflection that emerges from it. While analyzing this—our—culture from a critical distance, we discover the distinct constellation that, as a historical result, determines the context of our departure. Among the elements in which our thoughts are rooted, some have been particularly stressed by philosophers. More than their ancient, medieval, and modern predecessors, they concentrated not only on the conceptual structures, like the moderns, but were also and more concentrated on the linguistic, imaginative, social, historical, and libidinal processes we share as children of a certain time and space. Some authors have defended the exaggerated thesis that thoughts are only symptoms or effects of anonymous and "objective" instances, which they, according to their favorite perspectives, named "History," "Language," "The Unconscious," "Class," "Metaphysics," or "Violence." But who truly believes that the best thinkers really are no more than voices of such Neuters? Are these nameless powers the new gods we should praise or curse?

If we were mere effects or symptoms, how then would we be capable of discovering that we are permeated by such anonymous powers? Doesn't the very naming presuppose a distance that frees us from their might? The very awareness of our being determined by unchosen structures and mechanisms, and a fortiori the reflection upon their and our own nature, changes our dependence on the Anonymous and thereby its very character. Having lost our first naïveté, we cannot avoid taking a stance toward the fact of our being immersed and determined. We cannot continue to speak, behave, or be as we were, behaved, and spoke before our discovery of their influence. We have become different, because acceptance and rejection, struggle and transformation, have added a certain twist of our own to the anonymous powers that rule our lives.

The possibility of hermeneutics implies not only a distance from which we can look back and down upon our being involved in an unchosen but shared past and present but also a capacity for critical appropriation and at least a weak form of originality-through-transformation. In philosophy, this means that, as thinkers, we are able to convert a common heritage, including the traditions in which we are educated, into a new, personalized version of the Anonymous. The proof of this ability lies in the inimitable style of each one's personal mixture of appropriation, rejection, and transformation. As an indefinable touch of originality, a style cannot be captured by general concepts, although some of its features may be specified. Like fingerprints, this trace of a monadic author cannot be replaced but only counterfeited by epigones.

The originality of all transformations marks each hermeneutical treatment of the past as a renovation. A high degree of originality has been explained as the result of genius, inspiration, some voice from the outside, or some other force that is neither wholly common nor the author's private property. When a widespread belief in inspiration faded, veneration of the singular author became more intense—even to the point of declaring that the mere act of publication, regardless of the banal content, generates a copyright, for which only the author must be remunerated. One may guess that this laughable form of individualization belongs to typically bourgeois societies, whereas societies with more appreciation for the value of tradition show much less passion with regard to individual fame in cultural affairs. In any case, the originality of singular geniuses has not always been venerated as more important than the most tested parts of traditional wisdom.

The hermeneutical constellation of philosophy thus seems to imply at least three moments: the *thinker,* the *heritage* in which he finds himself rooted, and a *spirit* or *voice* responsible for the author's capacity to achieve a renewal.

Aside from the different versions and effects of the anonymous elements that constitute our cultural legacy, the past of a philosopher encompasses a series of classics. In this respect, the present actuality of philosophy is a retrieval that opens up a future by not being a simple repetition of the same. This kind of fecundation occurs in mainly two ways: (1) an original way of reading that is neither boring nor a total surprise, and (2) the faithful, historically correct, but not anachronistic reconstruction of the meaning expressed in the available texts, which thereby become accessible and, through the acquisition of new voices, continue to be part of a historical heritage. Without these ways of dealing with inherited texts, they would be reduced to a series of fossils, inhumated in the tombs of a dying or dead civilization. In order to play a role—i.e., in order to make a philosophical present possible—they must be saved from death by being resurrected again and again. To liberate them from the libraries and computers in which they are buried demands actual thinkers who grant them a new soul by providing them with words and practices of later times. The true university is *not* a collection of books and readers but rather an animated space in which spiritual fecundity is proved by surprising forms of reanimation. Immersed in but newly arising from its heritage, a living thought infuses an as yet unfamiliar life to bodies that would fall to dust without such inspiration.

If philosophical thinking is structured in this way, then philosophy itself *is* a history. This thesis destroys the possibility of a clear distinction between thematic (or contemporary) philosophy and the history of philosophy's past. They cannot be separated as two disciplines that should be practiced by different people or by the same person at different times.[3] Of course, it remains an urgent task to concentrate repeatedly and for many hours on close reading of inherited highlights. The careful reconstruction of their meaning would, however, lack all philosophical interest if we isolated it from actual questions at once similar to and different from those treated by their authors. Why should we bother about the thoughts of our prehistory, if this has become obsolete or unthinkable for us?

A certain form of estrangement is indispensable if we are to escape from the sickening repetitions of the dominant fashions proper to "our time." Since Parmenides and Plato, many specialists of thought and experience have stressed the necessity of arduous journeys and ascensions. Certainly Abraham, Moses, Jesus, and Paul, along with Parmenides, Heraclitus, and Plato, knew very well that the adventures of an exodus are indispensable for those who want to be freed from the ideological reflexes by which even the most sublime dimensions of human existence are threatened. Like prophets, great thinkers abandon the soil in which they are rooted like trees along a river, in order to risk their lives in deserts or exiles, battles, and expropriations. They break through the barrier of their homeland's opinions and customs to meet with various sorts of languages, standards, strangers, respectable enemies, and ambassadors from other cultures. A wholesome alienation confronts them with more aggressive challenges than those of the current literature known by heart. The most severe kind of emigration—avoiding all touristic or colonial pseudointerest—is hardly good enough to intensify their encounters and make them fruitful for their own renewal.

But where do philosophers find the strength to endure the estrangement of the linguistic, imaginary, emotional, and conceptual challenges with which they have to cope in view of a freer stance toward their still being at home in traditions of their own? Are they strong enough to endure the shocks caused by profoundly different revelations? If so, we still would ask: whence do they get enough energy and inspiration to come to terms with alien thoughts and intuitions?

Before we try to answer such questions, an additional remark may be useful with regard to the expression "our past," which has been used in the preceding pages. By recalling our common participation in "the Anonymous," including our philosophical legacy, we must realize that our past has never been closed and never can be closed, as if it were a well-defined fund, the totality of which could be described once and for all. The past does not exist apart from our reclaiming it. Our way of transforming it into a meaningful element of the future is an essential part of its constitution. In the history of philosophy, there "are" as many possible pasts as there are plausible re-presentations of it. The standard textbooks, for example, show by their selection alone from which cultural perspective the authors, as members of a particular community, look at their heritage and how they intend to transmit it to the future. The question, "what is the *real* past behind all the 'subjective' versions of it?" cannot be answered. Even if it is a meaningful question, who would be able to answer it? Who knows all the relevant documents of philosophy's history, and who has sufficiently thought through them to offer us the truth of its past? The very concept of "the past" includes a *particular* present that is marked by a perspective of its own. Such a perspective can be shared by many, but (1) it does not exclude other perspectives; (2) as there are as many presents as there are individuals, there are also different pasts; and (3) all presents and pasts are constantly changing. Indeed, there is no fixed and homogenous present but only a plurality of presents according to the different ways in which different people are connected to their reclaimed pasts. Some contemporary philosophers feel themselves closer to Plato than to Wittgenstein, others' thoughts are more medieval than Nietzschean, but who would be so pretentious as to forbid a colleague to see other ancestors and traditions as more central, promising, final, or crucial as others?

Those who reduce the history of philosophy to a standard series of classics commit the same error as those who isolate the anonymous instances of Language, Society, or Culture. By cutting them off from our present personal thinking, they identify the past with a realm of death and its productions with a museum of relics. The exhibition of fossils in libraries and other museums, where they can be studied in their most "authentic" fixity, might illustrate a preference for dissectible corpses over adventurous exploration of living possibilities, as does an obsessive insistence on prespiritual structures against the risks of fecundity and hope. Being fascinated with fossils paralyzes the present. But the very selection of relevant inscriptions already testifies to the irreducible power of germinal originality. Through selection, critical appropriation, and renewal, we *co*-determine the past whose children we are. The thinker is not his own father or mother but rather a re-creative recipient whose work hopefully contributes to a more lucid future.

FROM HERMENEUTICS TO DIALOGUE

Against those who tend to present anonymous forces such as Language, the Society, the Unconscious, or the Brain as overall principles of human civilization, the preceding pages have argued (1) that no form of "the Anonymous" produces anything at all if it is not taken up by subjects who, in their own original way, transform elements of it into new possibilities; and (2) that no preestablished power or system produces the individual thoughts that live from it, because the very constitution of Language, the Unconscious, Society, History, etc., presupposes a form of (co-)determination by those very subjects.

These statements do not fully answer the question of where and how a human subject finds the independence necessary to convert its participation in the Anonymous into an original future. Our initial immersion in an already existing style of life and thought is a sort of dream. Asleep, although full of images, phrases, behavioral reflexes, and so on, the subject is not yet a freely real subject. It lacks a minimal degree of selfhood; it is an instance rather than an individual. What can awaken it from this sleep to develop a stance and perspective of its own? Awakening cannot come from an anonymous Mother, if she does not want to let it go, nor from a real initiative of the fetus, since that would presuppose the awakening of birth. The emergence of autonomy needs the provocation of a third reality: an appealing "voice" different from the self-immersed murmuring that precedes responsible speech.

This leads us to the consideration of an element of the hermeneutic situation that is neglected too often: that any form of philosophical activity presupposes at least one other philosopher besides the one involved in thought.

A thorough analysis of the intersubjective aspects of philosophy presupposes an insight into the patterns of intersubjectivity on various prephilosophical levels. It is impossible here to present such a general theory, since most of it has yet to be discovered by original research. We cannot rely on undebatable results of generally accepted analyses that could then be applied to philosophical activity. I will therefore limit myself to some bold statements, whereas later chapters will propose more argumentation for the necessity of focusing on the dialogical relationship in philosophy and metaphilosophy.

The classical authors of modern philosophy from Descartes to Heidegger show little interest in the philosophical analysis of the encounter between you and me. If they wrote about intersubjectivity at all—and Kant, Hegel, Husserl, and Heidegger did, in connection with foundational problems of philosophy—they looked at it from the perspective of a philosophical ego that paid attention to a collective "we," which in their view was the concrete manifestation of epistemological or ontological universality.[4] However, without denying the importance of the common and collective aspects that bind philosophers together in a sort of "republic of thought,"[5] we must also stress that philosophical understanding—and human culture in general—involves an adequate account of the face-to-face relationships constitutive of all thinking.[6] Unilateral concentration on the common features that are presupposed in all forms of originality and shared by all of us as members of a particular society and time goes very well together with a one-sided accentuation of anonymous kinds of impact, but if we cannot show the irreducibility of face-to-face-relations within philosophy, neither can we save the critical distance nor the originality of individuals and their voices. Yet this distance and originality are essential in order to awaken individuals from their dreams.

A phenomenological description of the I-Thou relationship can begin with the observation that I certainly do *not* immediately and primarily perceive another individual—you or (s)he—as someone who is *similar* to me. When, for example, I see that you look at me, your look does not appear as something similar or analogous to my looking at you or at anyone else I have ever perceived. I *cannot* see such a similarity because I never saw and never will see my own looking at (someone). I may have some knowledge or *experience* of my own looking at others, but it differs greatly from the ways in which I perceive their looks. When I observe my eyes in the mirror, I see their shape, color, shades of brightness, and so on but not their looking at someone. One's image in the mirror is not only a reversal from right to left; it is a half-dead and uninspired portrait of one's face, which no longer looks at anyone (because there is no one to look at; indeed, the image I look at is not me and certainly not me-as-looking-at-someone). The other's face is her or his facing me or looking at me. The fundamental difference between my perception of myself and my perception of the other extends to other appearances of myself. I am, for example, equally incapable of seeing myself walking as similar to another's walking. In looking at a picture or movie in which I am walking, I see only a past that has been detached from my actual observation and objectified as the person I was for others.

I can observe your anger in your intensely burning eyes and the fist you just raised, but if I concentrate my attention on the raising of my own fist or on looking into the mirror in order to discover how wild my eyes are, my anger is gone. However, I feel my anger from within: I am hot or very dry and tense, and I am going to explode. It is amazing that, notwithstanding such differences in perception, we are still capable of having certain noemata that give us the right to speak of a certain similarity or analogy between the others' and my own facing, walking, gesturing, speaking, and so on.

When, for example, you and I are attending a performance of Euripides' *Medea,* I experience myself as imaginatively engaged in and emotionally moved by the drama the actors are performing. I have forgotten that I am looking at the stage because, with the actors, I participate in the plot that is unfolding before us. While you, too, are captured by the play, I can detach my eyes from the scene in order to observe the intensity with which you are looking at the actors on stage and experiencing emotions that correspond to the events evoked. I suppose that my looking at your looking at the actors is in some respects similar to my looking at the stage, but it is also very different: (1) the actors play a role, thus becoming other persons, whereas you are yourself, and (2) the motivation of my concentration on the actors is different from my phenomenological observation of the way you look at them. The main point here is that my perception of *your* looking (at the actors) is radically different from the mode in which I am aware of *my* own looking at them. The latter (my looking at the actors) is an experience "from within," which does not coincide with a thematization of my attention, whereas I do thematize your looking and concentrate my eyes on it. In order to *see* my own look, I must fix it as a *past* for my self-observing self, either with the help of imagination, by reflecting on myself-as-I-was-while-absorbed-by-the-play, or by observing an "objective" reproduction (picture, painting, video, or description) of my own looking, a reproduction made by others.

With regard to myself, I cannot combine, in one and the same period of time, the intention through which I intuit another being (you or the stage) and the intention through which I concentrate on that intuition. Both my looking at the stage and my looking at your looking have become a (remote or near) past for my self-observation, whereas my observation of your observation of the actors can happen in one and the same present.

The discovery that you, like and "with" me, are "at work" (*bei-der-Arbeit*) in the world, involved in networks of signifying references between things that can be characterized as "handy" or "ready-at-hand" (*zuhanden*),[7] is always preceded by an experience in which our similarity is not yet given. The immediate experience of our relationship is the experience of a basic dissimilarity: at first we are not similar but different—though somehow and somewhat alike.

Our dissimilarity is of a very special kind, however. It is neither the difference of two species within one genus nor that of two instances of one species. It is the difference of a *correspondence* between you and me. You and I are not primarily members of one collective whole but two bodies or selves who, because of their difference, can fit together as separate but corresponding extremes of a face-to-face-relationship.

This formalistic formula demands extensive explanation, of which, however, in this context, I can give only some fragments.[8]

The appearance of another person comes to me as a surprise: it is an amazing and never completely fathomable or integratable provocation. It wakes me up from the naïve, narcissistic dream in which I have been caught, enjoying the world of anonymous elements and forces. Without the shock of this provocation, I would not be able to acquire any distance toward my being part of a world through needs and satisfactions, lacks, attempts to heal my wounds, and strategies to intensify my pleasures. A basic distance is made possible by the summoning voice that awakens or calls and summons me. If I allow this voice to reach me, the dream or drunkenness of my narcissism is broken.

Among other consequences, the end of narcissism implies that the Anonymous has found its enemy. The estrangement, which earlier in this chapter was called a necessary condition for the critical and (re-)creative transformation of the Anonymous's impact on me, presupposes and alerts our liberty: the liberty of acquiring a distance from self-absorption. It is the radically other, who forbids and—if I permit this interdiction to target me—impedes my persistence in egolatry. Without liberty, our common fate could not even become a human one.

The other's provocation changes my life: it is not the same before and after our encounter. Hegel expressed this well in his famous dialectic of the battle that leads to mastery and submission. Every move of one person forces the other to choose a particular response from a very limited range of alternatives. To get involved in a fight entails a transformation of the fighting persons; each of them is forced to realize one of two or three behavioral transformations. And this example can be generalized: when meeting another person, I discover that my liberty is not a universal openness in front of innumerable possibilities but rather the necessity of a "choice" among a very restricted and determinate set of responses.

By his mere appearance, the other confronts me with an alternative from which I cannot escape: by his look or word or voice I am summoned to make space for the other in the world, which from now on can no longer be my exclusive property. To ignore this summons is a refusal to let the other in.

At first appearance, another is not my equal but a claim to which I must respond. The specific form of responding or (cor)respondence that is demanded from me has an ethical significance. Insofar as I do not permit another to refute my monopoly of the world, I discover myself to be guilty. The appropriate answer to the claim of your eyes is hospitality. The intersubjective relation thus not only has the character of dissimilarity but also of an ethical *dissymmetry*. The other's "highness" orients my life, if I accept the duties it imposes on me. I would act in a criminal way, however, if I were to force other persons to give their life for me.

I know—although I cannot see it—that others must perceive me in a way that is similar to the prepredicative superiority I see in them, but this does not constitute a phenomenological or directly perceivable equality. Only in a further stage of "constitution" does the reciprocity or our dissymmetry become the basis for our collegiality as similar and equal members of one human community.

The acceptance of another's entrance into my world is the beginning of not only an ethical but also an ontological history. The refusal of that entrance lies at the root of violence. Acceptance creates a community of universal justice; the alternative is war.

THE RELEVANCE OF INTERSUBJECTIVITY FOR PHILOSOPHY

Finally, I come to the question announced in the title to this chapter: how relevant is the face-to-face relationship for first philosophy?

If philosophy is a solitary way of thinking in which one philosopher thinks or speaks in the name of all others, then these philosophers should agree with the perfect philosopher. Their truth should coincide with the truth of their perfect representative or be a further development of it. This idea, which has, in fact, the status of an ideal, is imperfectly concretized in the best thinkers that can be found in the history of philosophy. I presume that we can agree by stating that the perfect philosopher has never existed, but many philosophers seem to have found a close approximation of him or her in one of the classics. If the best thinker of all has produced texts in which all other approximations have been or can be integrated, we can only copy, quote, extend, or further develop what his or her texts contain. If, for instance, Parmenides, Proclus, Aquinas, or Hegel incorporate such a thinker, we do not need the history of their past, unless we are curious enough to write an archaeology of their works. As for the neo-Thomists or the neo-Hegelians who want to remain loyal to their hero, we could be interested in the question of whether they only faithfully paraphrase, explain, update, and apply without distortion or also creatively transform the admired heritage.

If, in an even more attenuated version of the perfect-thinker paradigm, we admit that we have received only tentative versions of the truth, we still might prefer one oeuvre—say, that of Aristotle or Kant—over all others and treat it as the most outstanding replacement of the ideal. A comparison with other classics could then still be interesting to the extent to which these might offer perspectives or theses that have not been perfectly captured by the one that we have adopted as the source of our main philosophical legacy.

The more we discover that other philosophers have unfolded some truths that we cannot find in our own favorite philosopher, the more we become aware of the necessity to consult their works as well. As long as we consider one text or collection of texts—or, for that matter, one school or -ism—to be the only good or best, we might look down on supplements to the philosophy we celebrate. What we ourselves write is then epigonal, but it is also useful, because accurate paraphrases, lucid explanations, faithful commentaries, deductions of consequences, refined argumentations, good translations, and eloquent popularizations facilitate the access of others to insights that *the* philosopher (*Philosophus*) has already formulated.

A history of philosophy that reduces 2,600 years to the emergence of one philosophical monopoly that is true or closer to the truth than all others can allow itself to forget the history it presents—unless some forgotten element of the past surprisingly is revitalized and transformed into an entirely new question or perspective. By contrast, a historian of philosophy who respects the plurality of worthwhile but quite different approximations cannot avoid asking what this plurality means and reveals with respect to the truth, which obviously "likes to hide." Even such a historian might still decide to concentrate on one or a few philosophers. For example, because she sees philosophy as a series of singular philosophers in competition with one another to be recognized as the winner. The outcome of such competition would then be relevant, insofar as we need an exemplary past for our own progress. If it is true that we cannot begin with nothing, because we are not able to create *ex nihilo*, let us follow a leader—if possible, the best! But if we try to be more than mere epigones, what does it mean to seek and follow an exemplary leader? Where will we find enough distance to begin anew while, at the same time, continuing the tradition of a responsible, thorough, and "first" philosophy, instead of only producing a variety of scholastic repetitions?

If it is true that a fruitful distance toward our immersion in the past cannot emerge unless we are awakened by someone who has already discovered how thinking can renew a tradition by changing its burden into an enticing promise, then we cannot become inspiring thinkers unless we find our Socrates: an original philosopher or a revolutionary interpreter of already given phenomena and texts. If all great and small Socrateses are absent or silent, however, a truly inspired soul would have to be a miraculous hermit who concentrates on the universe from the summit of his solitary mountain. Would such a hermit have the courage to descend (like Zarathustra) if he were not (like Nietzsche) supported by a library?

Even Plato, so early in philosophical history, was, perhaps, not quite faithful to his own birth into philosophy. Notwithstanding his beautiful analysis of philosophical pedagogy as a sublime form of fecundity,[9] he presented Socrates perhaps too often as a king of thought who reduced his interlocutors to the all too seductive role of answering "yes" or "no." What a pity that he did not challenge Socrates more often by confronting him not only with Anaxagoras,

Parmenides, and Zeno but also with Heraclitus or Empedocles! Those who did not obey the rules of the game set by the "ignorant" king of philosophy were perhaps too quickly seduced by his questioning to contest it with very different questions that also could have been asked.

Every would-be philosopher needs the voice of others who already are at home in the world of thought. This presupposes a plurality of traditions and the polyphonic history of friendly dialogues or hostile altercations. However, an awakening voice need not always come from a philosophical giant—a modest scholar may even be better, because initiation should not be too overwhelming or authoritarian. However, the challenge should be intense and passionate, because no thought—no question, even—comes to life if it is not driven by an appropriate pathos.

The realm of thought is a historical interaction between masters and pupils, who thereby are prepared to be masters of other pupils. The real subject of philosophy is the community of participants who are neither kings nor merely members of an anonymous mentality or quasi-we.[10] Forgetfulness of the authors who sleep behind the silenced outreach of their texts leads to expiration. If living thinkers lend them a new voice, however, they revive in unexpected conversations. The historical documents of philosophy lose their breath unless they acquire a new eloquence in the surprising voices of rethinkers who make them inspiring again, while struggling with others and themselves.

The fecundity of an inspired philosopher realizes itself by awakening others from dreams of self-sufficiency. Such irruptions shake the dearest assumptions, if these are neither well experienced nor interestingly transformed in discussion with contending seekers and thinkers. Refutation of seemingly obvious and solid opinions is painful for those who have built their homes on them, but without purification and transformation—implying self-correction and pain—no real progress in philosophy is possible. Estrangement is necessary to escape from the established orthodoxies. Even if a thinker is extremely inventive and original, he will not be capable of radical turns in the style of Plato's *epistrophè*, the prophets' *metanoia*, or Heidegger's *Kehre*, unless an unescapable summons confronts him from the outside. Was it not Socrates who freed Plato from the shackles that held him in the cave? In the *Politeia,* Plato may be alluding to that event when he says that the decisive turn is not possible without the beneficial "violence" by which the outsider, who has seen the light, turns the dreamer away from the fascinating screen of imitations.[11] The nonviolent pressure put by philosophers on their students is a noble form of ascetic rigor. It is the summoning surprise of an approach that at first may seem wholly improbable but that gradually, while struggling, reveals the greatness of its possibilities.

Hegel is the great example of a philosopher who tried to engage the struggle without softening the contradictions that others' voices imposed upon his thought. He listened to their interventions with great care, risking more than once the destruction of his own convictions. Still, from beginning to end, he felt himself protected by an absolute horizon regarding which he played the privileged role of Hermes. As a spark of the universal *logos,* he surpassed all its seeming deaths. Although he widened the horizon of Western philosophy by an admirable kind of universality, his horizon remained dogmatic. Between the choice of an all-conclusive monologue and the skeptical surrender of all truth to vanity, he did not keep a space open for a radical divergence of singular perspectives that resists all higher syntheses but might surpass these perspectives in an other than dialectical way: perhaps—hopefully!—through the hidden convergence of a wordless union. His identification of the truth through the reconciliation of all worthwhile voices in one final unison prevented him from practicing and interpreting philosophy as a truth-loving discussion of irreducibly diverging positions, none of which is either the truth itself or an unamendable moment of the all-encompassing human Absolute.

In studying the interpretations through which Aristotle, Descartes, Kant, Hegel, and many other classical thinkers came to terms with one another and their predecessors, we notice that several of them cause distortions to their interlocutors' thought and that such distortions often condition their integration into the works of the heirs. In philosophy, egoism is not only unjust but also false. One may try to defend distortions by claiming that hermeneutic twists only cause a "fortunate guilt" (*felix culpa*) on the way to better views, but would not a more careful listening, by doing less violence to the irreducible alterity of thinkers, result in more authentic, deep, and fair discussions? Would it not have led to a less colonial and more hospitable form of recognition regarding other civilizations and approaches to the truth? The true response to which we are provoked by historical voices seems to lie in a judicious engagement with many different proposals whose quality justifies the hope that all of them, if serious, converge, in some permanently hidden way, into the omnipresent truth that dominates and directs us by desire rather than by exhibition.

Instead of trying to replace the multiplicity of competing philosophies with one victorious monologue, it seems highly preferable to think of philosophy's history as a discordant polyphony that orients the reader toward an ultimate but never fully revealed concordance. On the way to such a hidden but suggested point of convergence, some rules can be formulated:

1. Do justice to other philosophers by carefully interpreting—as "scientifically" and "positivistically" as possible—what and how they experienced, lived, sought, and tried to think and write.
2. Permit your own life and thinking to be summoned by instances of radical confrontation and welcome the chance of being challenged by fierce critique.
3. Revise your own position by transforming it into a part of your response to other positions and expressions.
4. Ask other thinkers and their best interpreters how they would respond to your views and arguments.
5. Do not try to finish the history of philosophy by being the wisest or the last speaker or the writer of its concluding synthesis.

The philosophical practice is without end: every time I encounter another thinker—master, student, or colleague—I am challenged. Beware of the boring repetitions that characterize and spoil interminable monologues!

Even if we accept the fact of each philosopher's radical and irreducible uniqueness, there is an alternative to the choice between being a dogmatic king and an anarchic nihilist. Philosophical pluralism is possible without betrayal of the truth, if we not only understand but also participate in the history of philosophy as a passionate and experienced conversation of those who, through the differences of their communication, reach out to a truth they love and serve beyond human possession.

FOUR

Education: Responsive Tradition

Education is the basic activity through which civilizations assure their continuation. It presupposes educators and pupils who are able to communicate with one another. Belonging to historical communities similar enough to permit mutual understanding, they transmit a specific culture from generation to generation. The process of transmission has been called *paradosis, traditio, tradition,* giving or passing on to others what first has been received. Educators are good if they are good at handing on what they, as educated in their context, have received in order to help others in taking root. Because, as Herakleitos saw, nothing remains the same, transmission and tradition have their own rules of identity and change: time and again, a culturally determined heritage becomes new while remaining a version of the same. Educators initiate their pupils into the culture that has become their own, but, since their pupils' lives occupy another time, the latter's appropriation of the tradition changes it into a different one.

Teaching philosophy is only one example of transmission, but an elementary analysis of it, especially if its historical dimension is not obscured, can show a temporal structure that, *mutatis mutandis,* recurs in all or most other examples.

THE PASSING OF THE PAST

To be a teacher is to be involved in the transition of a *past,* through the *present* of teaching and learning, into a *future* in which the past continues its life, thanks to its renewal. This transition is accomplished during a present in which the past is taught. To present the past, one must be attentive to the student's needs. The teacher passes on what she formerly has learned about the culture in which she has been educated, but to do this well, that culture must have become an integral part of her own manners of life, taste, moods, and thought. At the same time, the teacher is aware that her own needs and her personal or professional mode of appropriation do not necessarily coincide with those of her students. First, each student is, like the teacher, a unique individual, and second, the particular culture in which the teacher feels at home is already engaged in changing into a—at least somewhat—different culture, in which the next generation will be at home. One of the factors that causes a continual transformation of the heritage that, through tradition and teaching, has come to us lies in the different uniqueness that singularizes every teacher and every student. This difference shows already in the way in which the transmission is received and accepted, for the reception of a tradition is not the simple filling of a void or its imprint on an entirely empty and passive soul but rather an attentive and actively responsive appropriation. That such a response follows the suggestion(s) implied in the quality of the offered gift and the mode of its passing on does not diminish the receiver's responsivity and the singularity of his style and depth or breadth. Learning is itself an engagement whose modes range from obedience (which is a concentrated—and thus already self-determining—passivity) through a distanced interest to energetic appropriation. If the teacher's own past has not been driven by any active integration, she does not have much to offer. Then most of her work can be taken over by a book or a computer (which "knows" much more than she). Similarly, a student without passion for learning will not surpass the level of a correct but boring transmitter, and his version of received insights will be moribund. In other words, the available culture must be kept alive by the concerned tradition of its life through communication between already involved participants, one of which—the teacher—symbolizes and re-presents the past, whereas the other—the learner—will re-present it in the near future. Both are links in the extension of the past into a future that saves but also changes the past through the alchemy of teaching and learning that fills the present. A fruitful intermingling of teaching and learning presupposes that those who are involved share one temporality, although, as belonging to different generations, they live in different times and cultures. Tradition is the name of a shared temporality—a temporality that permits an unbreakable combination of repetition and renewal, loyalty and dissidence, or maintenance and transfiguration of the same.

TRADITION AS MEMORY

If education is the transmission of a culture's tradition from one generation to the next, educators are charged with the highest kind of responsibility to continue and renovate human history. In fact, a culture is not just the passing of one single tradition, nor even the totality of several traditions that cohere as components of a synthetic history. We are lured and besieged by a multiplicity of traditions, trends, and streams that may enclose us in a confusing form of confluence. This confluence has a physiognomy of its own, which often is simplified by calling it the ethos of an epoch. It gathers not only generalized opinions and popular convictions but also shared tastes and prejudices whose decency should not be doubted. If a particular epoch is distinguished by a characteristic ethos, each epoch would represent a specific mode of presenting the results—the heritage or the treasure—of one broad ongoing tradition. A picture of the way in which the European tradition (as the confluence of Greek, Roman, and other traditions) was effective in the thirteenth century, for example, is quite different from the presence of that encompassing but repeatedly modified and reinterpreted tradition in the seventeenth century. Apparently, these different epochs present different retrievals of a common past.

Trying to describe the overall climate of an entire epoch might be much too ambitious, however, even for a good historian—and certainly for philosophers, who always are inclined to overly simplify the character of collective phenomena. It is safer to narrow one's focus to one of the traditions that characterize a particular town, a region, a social class, a religious movement, or a professional association and to keep within a bounded period of time. Since we are particularly interested in philosophy, I will turn my attention to the question of what role is played by the philosophical tradition in today's education of philosophers.

Some philosophers hold the tradition of philosophy in rather low esteem. Some think that they can ignore it—even while they are sometimes reinventing very old wheels. Others are outspoken about the end of philosophy, and still others reduce the philosophical past to a classification of -isms. Almost everyone, however, loves and praises what is new and original, but whether the new has a better chance of being closer to the truth than the old—that is not often discussed. Neither is the boredom caused by certain forms of the ongoing philosophy often diagnosed. Is it perhaps a lack of passion and serious engagement that fails to awaken great excitement?

With regard to old traditions in philosophy, there are philosophers who show their condescension by calling them outdated, but others find new inspiration in close reading of the classics, showing how they can be revived in highly contemporaneous and exciting ways. Are the best attempts of such retrievals less new and farther from the truth than the newest proposals that—as so many revolutions of the past—have turned out to be less solid or profound than they initially seemed to be?

That the transmission of old attempts at formulating truth does play a role in contemporary philosophy can be demonstrated by spotting the multiplicity of implicit quotes from classical texts, even in the writings of those who don't care for historical studies. Another proof is found in the fact that each new essay refers to former essays, in which much has been said that must be remembered to understand the newer one. At least some segments of past history are always and necessarily present in philosophy.

It is, of course, not a revelation to state that thinking is impossible without *memory*. If an introduction into philosophy necessarily coincides with an appropriation of already existing traditions, then education in philosophy enables a student to participate in a collective remembrance of many experiments, paths, results, formulations, and perspectives that have been tried out and tested during 2,600 years of philosophical practice. To focus on this aspect of introductions to philosophy expresses the conviction that the history of thought is an integral part of philosophical practice. But then it is also extremely important that a student receive correct and sufficient information about our collective memory. Without an intimate familiarity with any tradition, a philosopher will not proceed very far. Thinking without remembering—or on the basis of strictly individual experiences and experiments—yields only stammering. Every interesting attempt at a new beginning (remember, for instance, Descartes, Spinoza, Kant, Fichte, and Hegel) presupposes serious wrestling with preceding traditions that must be surpassed or amended by a new one.

HISTORY AS MEMORY

What is the content and style of the memory that departments of philosophy offer to their teachers and students today? An answer to this question could begin by examining the widely accepted articulation of philosophy's history in American departments of philosophy.

If I am well informed, the works of the early thinkers that are sloppily assembled under the label of "pre-Socratic philosophers" are rarely taught, but some works of Plato (428–348 B.C.E.) and Aristotle (384–322 B.C.E.) are read and sometimes praised but also criticized as the first giants of philosophy. Some illustrations of later Stoic, Skeptic, and Epicurean thought may be given, but Middle- and neo-Platonism rarely receive attention. If Plotinus is treated seriously, at least three great thinkers of the one thousand years that separate Parmenides from Proclus (412–485 C.E.) are honored as fathers of the Western tradition and our shared philosophical memory. If the Greek and Hellenist development of Plato's heritage is left out, then the almost seven hundred years between Aristotle and Augustine must seem almost empty of noticeable thought.

I do not know how many schools pay attention to the more than one thousand years of thought that we even more sloppily assemble under the almost meaningless descriptor "medieval," but I guess that there are not many who make its study obligatory except Catholic universities, which most often concentrate on Aquinas. However, even many of the latter do not seem convinced that Augustine, Dionysius, Scottus, Anselm, Abelard, Albert, Alexander, Thomas himself, Bonaventura, Hendrik, Scotus, Cusanus, and many other extremely sharp and rigorous thinkers are the equals in competence and originality of Spinoza, Leibniz, Kant, Hegel, and some postmodern philosophers. Most often, one thousand years of sustained thought and critical discussion are reduced to one or two courses on Augustine or Aquinas, without situating them in the huge landscape of a long period more often dismissed as too theological than celebrated for having philosophers comparable to the best of modernity.

The last five hundred years of Western philosophy are everywhere considered important, but here also the real history is reduced to a few geniuses whose works *we* confront with each other, even if their authors were not aware of the interlocutors we assign to them.

There is something odd about the period that separates us from the modern attempts at restarting philosophy, clearly exemplified by Descartes' *Discourse on Method* (1637). During the two centuries between its publication and Hegel's death (in 1831), modern philosophy thrived. Even some philosophers of the twentieth century see Kant or Hegel as the thinkers who accomplished the promises of modernity, but it is difficult to deny that the modern ideal broke down under the fierce attacks of Schopenhauer, Feuerbach, Marx, Nietzsche, Heidegger, Wittgenstein, and those who, in their traces, are called—

again with a characterless name—"postmodern" philosophers. Poets, painters, and composers had warned us even before philosophers announced the end of their business as usual. Within the academic practice, however, most professors and students continue to focus on modern—postmedieval but prepostmodern—questions and methods, whereas quite a number of them are also fascinated by various attempts at breaking loose from that tradition by exploring new tracks of pondering and discovering. That we no longer feel safe in the traditional culture but instead are wandering amid widely differing possibilities—and, according to some, fascinating aspects of "the impossible"—without being capable of establishing a common base is felt by all, especially by our students. But the overall academic system seems hardly touched by the crisis.

Historically, during periods of uncertainty, and especially when philosophy seemed to have lost its inspiration, Europe turned to the Ancients for new inspiration. Many renaissances of an idealized "Greece" have punctuated our history. After the Virgilian one and the Christian transformations of Platonic and Stoic legacies, the Carolingian renaissance and the Aristotelian one of the thirteenth century, almost every century saw a revitalization of Greece, which seemed to allow for many interpretations. Whether it was the Athens of Pericles, the revival of the tragic worldview, the romantic retrieval of neo-Platonism, or the Heideggerian interpretation of a pre-Platonic sense of mystery, these renewed attentions to "Greece" triggered new departures—sometimes even a new beginning of Western history. One of the exceptions is perhaps Descartes' call for a radical rupture with the tradition. Indeed, his new project was mainly inspired by modern sciences, although Euclid was of course still very present in Descartes' admiration for the role of mathematics, while Seneca and Epictetus linked his ethics to its Stoic roots.

If the standard history of philosophy, as roughly sketched above, is still part of an "orthodox" initiation into philosophy, we might ask whether the biases it expresses are due to pure scholarship or rather to a characteristic belief or faith. Whatever the answer is, students who register for philosophy receive the message that they should widen their memory by studying a particular selection of philosophers, because these and no others are acceptable and recommendable to modern practitioners: "Trust us, who assure you that this selection provides you with a solid basis. Then, think with and against these heroes of a tradition in which you now also become a link, and initiate others in the same tradition, to which perhaps a few new geniuses must be added."

EVALUATION OF THIS MEMORY

What is the justification for the selective map or calendar that thus informs a student about the greatest thinkers behind his teachers, the heroes to whom they must refer, and the works on which they will write their dissertations?

The reduction of ancient history to a few great works could trigger a long discussion about the worth of classical humanism. Many practical, scientific, linguistic, religious, and moral reasons can be given for the imminent disappearance of the Greek and Roman sources from our textbooks, but fortunately there are still schools that consider such a disappearance a disaster, at least for the study of history, literature, and philosophy.

The negligence regarding 1,500 years of medieval philosophy is even more serious and telling: the unwillingness or incapacity to acquaint students with the spiritual traditions of the Christian period of Western history clearly expresses a prejudice that many intellectuals of the eighteenth century found "enlightened." Parallel to the political emancipation from autocratic governments, which came to an explosive head in the French Revolution, there arose a philosophical and scientific revolt against the dominance of religious authorities and, especially, against the powerful dogmatism of the Catholic Church, which tried to keep an authoritarian hold not only on its educative institutions but also on political governments. Separation of politics and philosophy from religion, recognition of human rights, and democratization of the State became the watchwords. Philosophy should become the emancipated sovereign within its own domain.

Independence from faith through autonomy of thought is one of the most important aspects of modern philosophy.

Implicit in this revolt was the conviction that obedient philosophies had to be ignored or despised because they did not honor the code of independent and self-justified thought. Since the theories produced before Descartes were considered to be pseudotheologies or—worse!—masked superstitions, their production could no longer be counted as part of the philosophical history. Further docility toward Augustine, Anselm, Thomas, or Scotus would confuse or infect students by imprinting outdated ideas on their brains. From now on, loyalty to rational enlightenment—or rather, as Hegel loudly proclaimed, "faith in Reason"[1]—was the only basis one needed to become a genuine philosopher.

The Enlightenment has greatly succeeded in eliminating the political and cultural power of Christian institutions from public and academic life. Many, perhaps most, intellectuals of the Western world do not welcome Christian influences on their study programs. Theology is tolerated in specific schools, but the role of religion as intellectual guidance seems to have been replaced by some sort of philosophy, most often under the name of "ethics" or "values." If philosophers offer a course on religion in the margins of regular courses on logic, epistemology, philosophy of mind, ethics, and social philosophy, they will rely heavily on the social sciences.

In these circumstances, one cannot expect that many students, once they have become teachers, will be prepared to explain why and how religion and faith are essential for an intellectually mature and well-conducted life and, consequently, for a nonsuperficial philosophy.

There are many good reasons for the very widespread disinterest, aversion, irritation, or hostility toward religion, especially among the younger generations of our time. One cannot defend the boring, hypocritical, unintelligent, abusive, and outrageous words and deeds of certain Catholic and other Church leaders. Similar reproaches are, of course, deserved by some or many representatives of nonreligious institutions, but these representatives are less outspoken about their own spiritual authority and the holiness of their mission. Whatever the moral and religious judgment about such actions and declarations must be, those who turn to academic philosophy for existential guidance will not find what they seek, if their school remains silent about those philosophers who tried to integrate conceptual analyses into their existential concern about the art of living well and beautifully.

As Pierre Hadot has shown, Hellenic philosophy was not a cerebral hobby of some isolated, unworldly intellectuals; it was instead a combination of dialogical, meditative, but also emotional practice and guidance of individual and communal lives. It suffices to study the hierarchical articulation of Plato's *Politeia* to understand that one cannot be a true philosopher unless a corporeal and affective balance is reached through time-consuming stylization of the human body and its erotic energies. Not only conceptual accuracy but also proportion, measure, and good taste are the standards for music, dance, drama, and eloquence—and equally for mathematics, philosophical conversation, and dealing with the architecture of the cosmos in light of the all-orienting Good-and-Beautiful.

Much more than a smart intellectual, the ideal of the Platonic philosopher was a well-shaped and beautifully reshaped individual who, conscious of his responsibility and of the good fortune that had made him capable of being a philosopher, would challenge, form, and reform others with the help of philosophical argumentations before he would be rewarded with total concentration on the metaphysical delights of contemplation.

Similarly, Aristotle's ideal of the philosopher is someone whose *logos* beautifies his interaction with others and the world, so that he can crown the harmony of his well-proportioned manners with the *sophia* of thoughtful admiration for invisible and eternal realities.

Like Plato's Diotima, Aristotle sees *Eros* (Desire) as the driving and all-connecting force of the human cosmos. Through *Eros,* we are always already tied to that which moves the all by being Desired.[2] It drives us from one stage of desire to the next, at every stage hinting at new aspects and intimations of the ultimate Desirable. Indeed, "the" desired "Good" or "Beauty itself" or, in other words, "the Beloved" are neither beings (*onta, ousiai*) nor ideas. They attract from beyond the cosmos as insuperably surpassing it, separate, transcendent, and therefore also most intimate.

What Christian thinkers and spiritual guides early on began calling *philosophia,* and what they continued to call *philosophia* until the end of the twelfth century, could not have been developed without a transformation of the Platonic tradition they received from pagan texts and teachers. They recognized their own and all humans' Desire in Plato's *Eros,* while converting it into a new kind of seeking in response to a divine vocation. Thus *Eros* became a prefiguration of the circular love (*agapē*) that begins in the God of Abraham, Moses, and Jesus Christ in order to flow back through the shared and mutually enacted love of persons for one another toward that God who lives in them.

Across more than fifteen centuries, a proliferation of experiential, mystical, theological, and philosophical guides and descriptions was generated within the Christian history of that Love. From Paul and John to Cusanus, Pascal, Malebranche, and Blondel, the philosophical legacy of Plato, Aristotle, and Plotinus has been transmitted, interpreted, reinterpreted, and adjusted to the affective, imaginative, poetic, and theoretical conditions of the various epochs it traversed. What we moderns still can recognize as "philosophy" in it—if "philosophy" at all can be identified as the bare bones of sophisticated rationality—is there liberated from its narrow limits and lifted up to the fuller level of a life-embracing faith. Of course, it also has been associated and mixed with dated beliefs and practices. But how alive and inspiring has this Eros remained, even in its most sophisticated *quaestiones disputatae!*

RESPONDING

After my much too sketchy examination of today's standard history of philosophy, we must return to the question of philosophical education and the memory it must presuppose.

Through my teachers, who mediate between me, the student, and the giants of thought behind them, the latter also become my teachers and interlocutors. If Kant, for example, speaks to me through his texts as re-presented by one of his interpreters, it is not only the latter but Kant himself who challenges me to an unavoidable response. Once I allow Kant really to reach and touch me, I cannot fall silent. If I do not reduce his work to an "interesting" document but also read with him and recognize his voice as targeting me, I cannot stop at listening and appropriating his thoughts. They summon me to a thinking-in-response. Since true, i.e., passionate, thinking comes from the heart, however, Kant's exciting words demand a personal response from me, "personal" meaning here "one that only I can give." Kant's talking to me, paraphrased or explained by my teacher, makes me co-responsible for the question Kant is asking, although I might be forced by our and my own difference from Kant to reformulate and adjust that question. He makes me also responsible for his answer, insofar as I ignore, approve, reject, or amend it.

Plato, Aristotle, Augustine, Bonaventure, Kant, Hegel, and some others have become acquaintances whose words I remember with the assistance of their texts and my teachers. They seduced me to a sustained effort of struggling with their overwhelming thought. Slowly I became familiar with their style and the coherence of their approach. They became admired friends and, once in a while, I can predict how they would have answered a question about which I have found as yet no answer in the texts that I have read. My trust in the greatness or depth of their thought has not disappeared, but now I can give reasons of my own for why my trust was and remains justified. However, it is not true that my trust can be reduced to the logical conclusion of a well-built syllogism, because trust involves much more than reasoning. One of the features that belongs to philosophical greatness is that a thinker is more than a stupendous brain: the great philosopher is a teaching voice who deeply touches at least some of his or her students. Who are the teachers from whom we learned the most? Probably they are those philosophers whom we remember as admirable persons whose philosophical knowledge testifies to an inspired life and not only as specialists of conceptuality to whom we owe gratitude for their training in the required skills. A role model must have more than astonishing erudition. For example, it also presupposes a successful integration of thinking into the whole of this unique individuality—into, that is, the corporeal, emotional, imaginative, dialogical, and communal aspects of my teacher's irreplaceable humanity.

In the course of my struggle with some hero of mine, a phase might occur in which my thought becomes almost identical with that of my admired or even befriended philosopher, but identification, if possible at all, is not what they or I would like, because it would not be entirely genuine. A radical but not unfriendly distance remains, not only because time, culture, history, and situation separate me from all exemplary thinkers but primarily because, like them, I, too, am singularly unique, even if I cannot compete with theirs. In my own way, I am responsive for my thinking, thanks to their summoning me, and this makes me a part of the tradition in which we celebrate their resurrection, thanks to the respondents whose loyalty also changes their legacy.

It would not be very difficult to show in detail how Plato lives and thinks again in many of his greater and lesser heirs, but there are many degrees of loyalty and affinity to him among them. A full response to his oeuvre cannot be limited to a cerebral rechecking of the logical or epistemological correctness of Socrates' sentences—especially not if the reader has already decided that Hegel or Frege or Heidegger is the standard.

Responsivity in a Platonic style would involve the responder in more than logically correct forms and interesting theories. Platonic responsivity also illustrates how, in responding to challenging texts, passions and emotions get harmoniously intertwined with corporeal and cordial energies and how intuition (*nous*), paired with good sense (*phronēsis*) or taste (*aisthēsis tis*), is indispensable for the emergence of a well-disposed stance. Above all, it shows that the way—or method—of philosophy is an incessant ascent toward the absolute, which is beyond comparison, although we may point at it with names that evoke nothing specific or generic but rather Beauty itself, the Good, or the One. A philosophical ascent in a Platonic style thus proceeds in many stages toward that One, but it remains without a *definable* end.

If not only the Platonic but also the Christian tradition of *philosophia* is taught, one will discover how many Platonic features of philosophy are integrated into differently loyal transformations, like those of Gregory of Nyssa, Augustine, Dionysius, Bonaventura, Thomas, Scotus, or Cusanus. The integration of thinking and dialogue; the mutually adjusted inclusion of thought, affectivity, imagination, calculation, corporeal health, and beauty; the reaching out and the patient, cathartic, and austere but delightful and adventurous seeking of the Good beyond all gods—all of these transformations are recognizably Greek and Platonic, but at the same time they are ennobled by their integration into a faith that, as the highest expression of a grace-given history, continues to bless whatever is worthy of serious trust and praise.

How can we say that the Good and its ungraspable proximity is absolutely trustworthy? Because we are already "in touch" with it and tied to it—not by seeing, hearing, or feeling but by *Eros,* Desire.

In reaching out, the Desire that drives us is always already "touched" by and aware of the only One who is Desirable beyond all desirability, although we most often do not know it. "Touch" and "awareness" are here, of course, metaphors, but the mystics are able to describe its experiential authenticity. The heart of ultimate trust is the certainty that the core of Desire reaches out beyond the splendor of the universe and that this reaching out is not in vain. What human existence from the beginning desires—the Desired that makes sense—is lovable. Ultimate trust holds that underneath—and within—the many, often misleading drives and confusions that obsess our sensuous, affective, and intellectual struggles we are anchored in One, whose intimate but restlessly motivating presence is felt as the only Desirable without fail.

Responsivity and responsibility for the traditions of which we already are or still must become the teachers demand that we are inspired by a pathos that has overcome at least a certain degree of being inhibited by the *pleonexia* of incentives whose monstrous harassment results in making us tyrants. Plato defined human evil as the turning upside down of a genuine philosopher. Christians would rather interpret evil as arrogance, *superbia,* pride. However, without erasing the considerable difference between Plato and Christian philosophers like Augustine, we must recognize a deep affinity between their attempts to identify the primary source of movement as a pathos that nobody can choose, because it has already chosen us in order to give us an orientation and final address.

How does Desire work in dealing with the heroes and traditions of philosophy? How does it give guidance to students and teachers for finding their way among the paradigms of a truly representative history of philosophy? Is *Eros,* as reaching out to the Good itself, sufficient for guiding our participation in the best of philosophical traditions? No. The glory of the Good-and-Beautiful or the Desirable itself is too infinite and too absolute to allow for any deduction of its concrete configuration. However, as the memory of more or less fortunate attempts at articulating credible maps of the universe, the history of philosophy invites us to a journey of discovery. Is there any scientific, logical, moral, or aesthetic rule that can guide us on this journey?

In his first philosophical publication, Hegel makes the ironic remark that some philosophers behave like Adam, who let all kinds of animals pass before his eyes in order to give an appropriate name to each of them.[3] The philosopher arranges a procession of philosophies in order to classify them as a sequence of -isms. In his *Phenomenology of Spirit* (1806), which he called his "explorations" (*Entdeckungsreisen*), Hegel himself celebrates a parade of all the philosophies he esteemed worthy to take a place of honor in the orderly preparation of final transparency. The standard that enabled him to organize his parade was *Reason*: the power of conceptual analysis, synthesis, and totalization.

We have lost that standard, because we have lost faith in Reason's totalitarian omnipotence. Reason is no longer independent from Eros and Pathos in general. We no longer believe that history is an unstoppable progress from primitive stammering to the most splendid triumph over all finite positions and negations. We can no longer deduce the sequence of philosophical constellations. Our memory no longer has the character of a logically necessary genealogy. However, another trust can replace Hegel's faith in reason, without robbing reason of its claims to coherence within the realm of totality.

If Desire moves because the absolutely Desirable attracts us, it is our task to identify those philosophies that offer a foretaste of ultimate lovability. The religious literature of East and West offers many descriptions of ladders, ascents, mountain climbs, travel guides, and journeys that lead from stage to stage through configurations of love and being loved. Some of those guides are highly sophisticated. The most philosophical of them is probably Bonaventure's *Itinerary of the Mind into God,* which all by itself demonstrates that nothing impedes *philosophia* from being at the same time very philosophical and a hymn of love to Love.

A good discernment of the approximations and alienations that are experienced in visiting the great teachers of our past presupposes a progressive *katharsis* of the traveler's sense for genuine goodness and beauty. What *katharsis* means and how one ought to engage in it has been described by many guides of purification in all religions, including the religious parts of ancient and medieval philosophy. Many masks and distortions of the absolute Desire emerge along the ways that lead toward the true Desirable, because human desire generates a host of imitations that present themselves as absolutes. Honor, fame, pleasure, money, mastery, arrogance, and pride beg for limitless love, but they would suffocate Eros were not the One infinitely Desirable somehow announcing its delayed but unstoppable approach to the traveler, whose falling in love with the Beloved has its beginning in an immemorial past.

FIVE

Philosophy: Wise about Friendship?

In memory of André Schuwer

To broach a discussion about the relationships between *philosophy* and *friendship*, I begin by asking: to what extent should friendship play a role in philosophy, and to what extent can philosophy play a role in friendship?

If friendship is a topic of ethics, and if a reflection on the practice and theory of philosophy constitutes a metaphilosophy, a meditation on the relations between philosophy and friendship belongs to the ethical part of metaphilosophy or the metaethical part of ethics. As Plato, Aristotle, Kant, and Hegel are still teaching us, ethical considerations remain too abstract if they are not preceded and followed by (1) an analysis of the social and political situation from which ethical questions emerge and (2) an examination of the connections that bind our virtues to the various dimensions of *philia*. Let's therefore begin with a brief description of philosophy as a social practice that has its own political conditions, in order thereafter to focus on some ethical aspects of the more or less friendly kinds of exchange between philosophers.

PHILOSOPHY

According to the *Historisches Wörterbuch der Philosophie* (vol. 7, col. 573–576), the words *philosophos* and *philosophein* originally expressed the *philia* (friendship or love) characteristic of those who enjoy the presence of *sophia*. The meaning of *sophia* in this context encompassed several kinds of knowing, from technical expertise to wisdom. Early on, *philosophia* was not restricted to the sort of investigation practiced by Plato or Aristotle and certainly not to the type of argumentation that modern philosophers have privileged over other paths to knowledge or wisdom. The ancient love of wisdom has changed into the modern pursuit of demonstrable truth, but this redirection of philosophical inquiry has been frustrated by so many contradictions and disappointments that many philosophers now see uncontaminated truth as unattainable for mortal minds. Those of us who are convinced that truth seldom shows up in full glory, without however falling into complete despair, might prefer to replace the words "love" and "friendship" (*philia*) in our translations of *philosophia* by "desire." This would bring us closer to its Dutch translation: *wijsbegeerte* (*desire* of *becoming* wise)—even if pure and perfect wisdom turns out to be an impossibility. Notwithstanding the imperfect and constantly deferring character of philosophy, however, desire has involved us in a historical search for the truth itself, which testifies to our very deep interest in it. Passion for truth has inducted us into a world where we are simultaneously at home and still underway. Though not yet wise, we are already affected, even wounded, by the truth, whose promising proximity remains distant, while seducing us by showing glimpses of its blinding purity.

Desire has the eschatological structure of an unfulfillable but productive promise.[1] It instigates a time of growing familiarization with partial appearances of the truth, but it does not guarantee any full *apocalypse*. If we were absolutely separated from the truth, we could not be at home in philosophy or even underway. An almost blind trust and the hope that thinking and rethinking, even without resulting in final proofs, will make us wiser and guide our search. Hence, we rely on our inchoative and eschatological "being-in-the-(as-yet-hidden)-truth" through endlessly renewed attempts at encountering its embrace.

The social structure of our being-toward-and-already-in-the-truth might perhaps be described in the following way. As philosophers, we participate in a worldwide endeavor shared by many travelers who learn, repeat, and modify the practices of a community with the history and actual unfolding of which we are more or less acquainted. This community encompasses a great variety of subcommunities, associations, schools, and styles, but all are held together by a certain affinity, even if we cannot detect a uniform system or some basic principles that are common to all philosophers. As members of the philosophical republic, we are heirs to a huge heritage, of which we know no more than some fragments and decisive events. The tradition through which we remain connected with a generous past has its own heroes, documents, discoveries and inventions, wars and victories, commentaries and retrievals, memorials and revolutions. As participants in the philosophical community, we play various roles according to our affiliation and capabilities, each having a particular style of analyzing, discussing, teaching, proposing, and experimenting. Concerning our relations to this community, three important questions, among others, can be asked:

1. What are the primary institutions through which philosophy regulates the philosopher's thought and life?
2. How does one become a philosopher and member of this republic?
3. What binds us together as philosophers, gathering us up into one community?

If the first question asks for a description of the social and political structure of the philosophical enterprise, the second concerns the genealogical elements that determine the activity of individual philosophers, and the third question asks how political and historical settings condition their interpersonal commerce. Obviously, a satisfactory answer to these questions would involve a huge interdisciplinary study of the sociological, political, and psychological aspects of the quest, in combination with a far-reaching competence in philosophy. Instead, I can offer here only a few suggestions for the execution of such a project.

INSTITUTIONS OF THE PHILOSOPHICAL REPUBLIC

Even if philosophy is of common concern to all philosophers, the comparison with a commonwealth or republic seems misguided, because the philosophical community obviously possesses neither a government nor any unifying power other than the ideality of its truth. However, philosophers remember great founders, appeal to certain authorities, celebrate decisive events, cultivate traditions, and submit to specific rules and judges. It is true that the influence of their heroes is only ideological, and different schools cherish different lists of exemplary thinkers (there are, for example, those who do not look up to Plato but venerate Nietzsche, and those who despise Heidegger but admire Carnap), but in each epoch, there still seems to exist enough consensus about a core group of classics to express a widely shared recognition of their importance. In addition to its standard texts, philosophy also shares a common language and logic, although the different dialects of competing parties frequently obscure their underlying agreement.

Besides its exemplary thinkers, philosophy also has its managers. Quite a number of philosophers have become chairpersons of university departments, leaders of teaching projects, directors of research centers, administrators of associations, organizers of congresses, or planners of meetings where the practitioners present and discuss their own ideas. Quite often the managers were or continue to be prolific teachers and writers or outstanding researchers, but their managerial tasks do not always allow them to be fully updated in the philosophical processes they serve.

A more detailed analysis of the structures that govern today's philosophy would presumably show a rather diffuse and shifting distribution of power among the participants. Thus a quasi-political structure would become visible and a history of philosophical politics could be written. While a Hobbesian "state of nature" is rare among philosophers, they have not organized a body politic ruled by a superphilosophical king or counsel of the wise, but it would be naïve to ignore the role of informal power in the history of philosophy, for example with regard to success and fame.[2]

In contrast with the absence of generally recognized or elected rulers, the commonwealth of thinkers recognizes certain standards for good work, which are applied by judges, of which philosophy has plenty. In hiring and granting fellowships, many evaluators and decision makers are involved; in reviewing and publishing texts there may be fewer, but almost all philosophers have been evaluated, appointed, or dismissed, praised or blamed several times in their professional lives.

Within the philosophical republic, several schools have formed, most often around or in the aftermath of an original or influential thinker, who can be seen as a founding father or mother. Schools have their own orthodoxy and particular systems of standard assumptions and prohibitions, besides the universal rules about method, logic, and rhetoric recognized by all. The same can be said of the epochs of philosophical history. Few to none of our philosophical journals, for instance, would publish Heraclitus's dicta or St. Augustine's *Soliloquia,* and the orthodoxy of some twenty-first-century schools excludes all contamination by Heideggerian literature or theological interests.

Philosophy has not only its own trends and trendsetters, media and marketing, but also its characteristic liturgies. Most of these liturgies are no more than a series of monologues, followed by questions and answers that leave everything as it is. If such gatherings were a faithful picture of life in the philosophical community, one could conclude that it is a marketplace where individuals show how competent they are with an eye to being known, heard, hired, honored, promoted, admired, invited, remunerated, and so on. What is common to all of these individuals who approach one another as solitary thinkers who hope to find recognition and inspiring response? Of course, such gatherings also offer opportunities for setting up cooperative projects, facilitating discussions or conspiracies, and other kinds of politics, but are these expressions of commonality central to philosophy or merely marginal, sometimes perhaps even opposed to its essential purpose?

These quick indications may suffice to set the stage for an examination of the way in which philosophers should behave with regard to one another. An ethics of philosophy can begin by focusing on the responsibility of philosophers for themselves and others, insofar as all of them are supposed to be underway to truth. A common cause rules over this responsibility; it is the real center of their commonwealth. It asks for dedication, discernment, and well-oriented interest—an interest that everyone can share without falling into conflicts of interest. An ethics of philosophical responsibility would, for example, point out how serious and difficult the task of a reviewer is in judging the work of another philosopher and which virtues (such as justice and humility) are the necessary conditions for fair discernment. Such an ethics would also draw the line between devotion to truth, on the one hand, and the many forms of perversion and corruption, motivated by narcissism, greed, will to power, or vanity, on the other. It would show that loss of all faith in the possibility of truth necessarily results in a replacement of the main interest by goals other than truth, thereby triggering a war between the thinkers who adore those divisive goals. If such goals become idols, the philosophical republic falls apart—because greed, love of power, addiction to pleasure, and obsession with personal fame divide, if they are not kept in place and humbled by the truth.

INITIATION

To answer the ethical question of how a philosopher should move within the philosophical community to be good as a thinker in company with other seekers after truth, we might have a look at the way that one becomes a philosopher. Initiation, learning, and maturation presuppose guidance and growth. Nobody is born a philosopher; everyone is educated before becoming an heir of our legacy. Each of us has been introduced to philosophy by teachers who represented the available abundance of thought by offering us a share in their selective appropriation of well-formulated questions and attempted answers. We have learned how to integrate and renew the thinking that others have documented before us, but no existing philosopher has ever comprehended the entire wealth of knowledge that is available in our libraries and traditions. Each teacher is selective and partial, possessing only a particular body of knowledge and a characteristic manner of managing it, but even if 90 percent of our sentences or more consists of quotes, something in our discourses is unique and irreplaceable. In rethinking what already has been thought, it is the uniqueness of the new performer that counts—a uniqueness that does not coincide with yet is expressed in the rhetorical and conceptual elements of the performer's speech or writing.

The analogy between the rethinking of traditional thought and the live performance of a musical score might illustrate the difference between philosophy in the sense of an available treasure and the actual philosophizing of those who transform that treasure into a new event. Comparable to musicians who bring soundless scores to new life, genuine philosophers recreate a great deal of shelved thought as part of their renovation through teaching and interpretation. Good teachers know how to train their students in a retrieval of given texts. At the same time, however, they limit the given treasure to those parts of it with which they are well acquainted. If students have several teachers who propose contradictory perspectives to them, they are forced to choose among the different proposals, or to reconcile them (which demands real mastery), or else to postpone a decision about their adherence to any of the proposed approaches. Although few students will cause a revolution, all of them must find their own style of transformation, even if their greatest strength may still lie in quoting, paraphrasing, or commenting. In any case, the patient labor of faithful reconstruction—which, of course, implies a great deal of repetition—is necessary to represent the traditions without which the philosophical community could neither exist nor occasion the emergence of surprising originality.

The main point I am trying to make here is that individual philosophers owe much of their thinking to others: to the teachers, who bring elements of our common heritage to life; to the authors, whose texts they decipher; to the still living thinkers, whose admirable work challenges them; and to their students, whose reactions force them to clarify and correct their own thoughts before being able to teach them. From the very beginning of thinking, each of us is involved in the social relations of a historical and contemporary network of ongoing thinking within a very large historical community. Teachers and other predecessors deserve gratitude for our participation, and colleagues invite cooperation while challenging us by inventive proposals, appetizing hints, or bold assertions that prompt us to amendments or partial refutation. Social relations in philosophy sustain the life of a community that, if uncorrupted, promotes mutual attention and discussion.

WHAT BINDS PHILOSOPHERS?

If no one can become a philosopher without initiation and education, i.e., without a kind of rebirth and growth in the world of thought, then philosophers are not autarkic as long as they still have to learn. Is it at all possible to reach a state of consummate wisdom, or do we always remain dependent upon other members of the philosophical community? Can individual philosophers be autonomous, or is their work conditioned by the conversation to which they belong as interlocutors, without ever becoming wholly sovereign? If the latter is true, then what binds these interlocutors together?

The modern conception of the philosopher as an autonomous *Cogito* implies that the philosophical republic is structured as an association of individuals who, though involved in an exchange of ideas, are capable of justifying all their truths on their own, even if they are not the first to discover them. Social relations may be necessary for the genealogy of their insight, but can't every sufficiently intelligent person acquire the same insights, once the proofs are clear? If truth is possible at all, the association of autonomous individuals in search of truth seems to promise a peaceful history. But why then does the reality show so much competition and contradiction or even hostility? Does not the truth unite those who are enlightened by it?

I see only four possible answers to this question: (1) either the competition among philosophers is caused by something other than love of truth; (2) the truth approaches us only in a variety of seductive disguises, to which some philosophers are more attached than to the (hidden) truth itself; (3) we must give up the postulate of individual autonomy; or (4) a combination of the preceding three answers.

1. The idea of competition is central to the social and political philosophy of ancients and moderns. Who doubts that tensions inevitably emerge between individuals who are primarily interested in their own survival, security, well-being, freedom, possession, power, fame, pleasure, and so on? All *these* interests are divisive, because either the desired goods are scarce or the interests are inflated, but it is not clear how *truth* can generate a war. People can dissent about the truth and they can also become impatient or angry about others' or their own lack of insight, but such conflicts do not lead to real fights so long as the interlocutors aim at the only and whole truth. Indeed, insight can be shared without causing envy. Since truth is universal, it cannot be possessed as an exclusive property. If seekers of truth fight with one another, they must be motivated by other interests, for example by a desire to be the first in publishing an idea that is not yet known, or by the desire to formulate some truth in an exceptionally brilliant way, or by the desire to impress their audience with a vision that appears pleasing or condoning. Such motivations would explain hostility, but they are extraphilosophical; if they prevail in the philosophical community, its degeneration is already well advanced.

2. The distinction between love of truth and other interests, as presented here, may be too clearly cut, however. If the truth itself always hides in its appearances and approximations, even when these disguise its presence, the temptation can be strong to identify

the truth with one of its imitations. If individual philosophers or schools succumb to this temptation, they are prone to proclaim their doctrine the only correct one, which then leads to battles with other philosophers. Moreover, if the adherents are fond of power, they will try to govern the entire community by imposing their doctrine or method as the universal code that all members must agree to apply. The end of Plato's *Republic* shows to what kind of tyranny such a caricature of truth in the end must lead.

3. As for the third answer to the question of how we can explain the competition among people who simultaneously profess the universality of truth and the autonomy of individual thought, we can probably agree that the idea of a fully autonomous consciousness represents a transcendent spirit rather than a human mind. If, for the purpose of the present meditation, we focus on the intersubjective conditions of thinking, we must get a clear idea of how philosophers belong to the existing community that enables them to philosophize the way they do. What does "belonging" in this context mean, and what unites the members who belong to that community?

At least two perspectives must be combined to answer this question. The first concentrates on all that philosophers *share* with one another, while the second points to the speaking and listening through which they, as interlocutors, *communicate* with one another. The first perspective exhibits the being-with (*Mitsein*) of philosophical solidarity, whereas the second accounts for the face to face relationship that binds different thinkers together even more strongly than their common concerns do.

It is obvious that philosophers share most of their information, literature, quotes, thoughts, methods, and behavior, despite individual variations and different degrees of originality. The task of searching for truth and developing discoveries that have been made creates a common interest, by distributing various roles and functions among the participants of the general movement. In the history of philosophy, we study the cultural aspects of this process. By showing that thinking is conditioned by traditions, texts, commentaries and interpretations, restructurings and revolutions, we explore the communal and historical dimensions of all thought, especially of its most original versions. In a hermeneutical context, the autonomy of individual thinkers risks being entirely dissolved into the preceding and surrounding processes to which they owe their inspiration. A certain independence remains essential, but its role and essence must be rethought in relation to the conditions that support and limit its liberty. One can point at the element of originality that is involved in all retrievals without denying the impossibility of a completely freestanding choice among thinkable alternatives; however, a more fundamental meaning of autonomy than the popular one is found in the responsibility that is implied in all face-to-face relationships between interlocutors.[3]

Before we analyze the relationship that connects two or more persons who *address* one another, a remark is needed about the perspective that allows us to speak or write about this relationship. To respect and do justice to the facing (or speaking or addressing) that relates persons, we should *avoid* the standpoint of a third uninvolved observer or the perspective of a Heideggerian I-in-the-world. Indeed, the uninvolved, neutral, panoramic, and transcendental point of view looks from above or from the outside at the facing, speaking, listening, and turning that relate you and me. Such a perspective prevents the observer from experiencing what happens between you and me, when we address each other. The neutral, "objective," uninvolved observer is blind with regard to the other's face qua *facing*. Insofar as your face faces me, your speech is directed to me or your letter addresses me; they affect and concern only *me*, the one who is faced, the addressee. The one who faces or speaks to me can only be someone in the position of (a) *you*.

With regard to Heidegger's being-in-the-world, its contrast with being-faced-and-facing demands a more complicated analysis, which I cannot give here.[4] Let it suffice for now to indicate that being-with (*Mitsein*) constitutes a certain solidarity between the persons involved, i.e., their forming a we; however, it neither structures nor characterizes the *face-to-face* of an encounter between you and me. *Fürsorge* is the consequence of a responsible being-*for*-and-*toward* you, but Heidegger does not found it in an originary *Existenzial* of its own, although it cannot be explained as a modification of the we- or *with*-structure. A phenomenology of "the face," if it is at all possible, cannot be written by someone who is not in the position of an addressee. Of course, while writing such a phenomenology, the writer is no longer completely fascinated by the facing or speaking to which he or she is listening. Her description is a lateral clarification of the interlocutory relation, and as such it already slips away from the experience she wants to evoke. As a description, it succeeds only to the extent to which she is able to maintain a double attention: at the same time that she faces the other, who is facing her, she must characterize the experience of this mutual facing ("you, whom I see, are facing me") as an encounter that unites the faced and facing other ("you") with her own ("my") facing and being faced. *Intimate* towardness (you and I) and at least some degree of describable togetherness ("with") must be combined in order to achieve a successful phenomenology of you-and-me. The double attention that is required here alternates between two perspectives rather than joining them into one simultaneous and transcendent or transcendental overview. It attempts to join the event *about* which we speak with the *to* or *toward* that is proper to the speaking-and-listening, which, in the event, relates you and me. Although this relation cannot be understood as an example of Hegel's dialectic, it is "dia-logic" insofar as it heeds the union of an irreducible difference without swallowing either term of the relationship.

The addressing structure of all greeting, gesturing, regarding, speaking, listening, writing, and reading is often neglected in metaphilosophical essays on the essence of philosophy. Yet the entire world and history of philosophy depends on it. All speeches, texts, or thoughts would be mute and dead—merely fossils—if they were not handed down and received by interlocutors who—as teachers and pupils, colleagues, or scholars in conversation—constantly turn their attention toward one another. The Aristotelian formula *legein ti kata tinos* might suffice to indicate the structure of a simple proposition,[5] but if we forget that all that is said presupposes *someone* who presents it to *someone*, we end up like ghosts amid a cemetery of insights awaiting their resurrection. *Language does not speak* unless someone takes responsibility for its use and unless a listener responds to it.[6] A proposition is always a proposal through which someone tries to attract, teach, enrich, critique, or seduce someone else. First and foremost, philosophy is a live conversation among philosophers who communicate with one another. In doing so, they count on mutual understanding insofar as they exploit a shared heritage, refer to a common canon, and use a common language (even if their language is broken into different dialects). But all these conditions are waiting for individual voices to be transformed into new thoughts that pass from you to me and from me to other "you's" and "we's." Texts can be compared to letters: if they function, a protracted correspondence may emerge.[7]

Addressing creates a bond. In speaking to me, you make me your respondent. I can refuse to listen or to answer your speech, but my silence too *is* a response. Often it is even more eloquent than an aggressive rebuttal. If I take your speech seriously, I am already involved in an exchange that might develop into a conversation. In philosophy, such conversations represent the living parts of the wider community. Because speaking and listening cannot exist without saying something about something, the contents of the exchange certainly are an essential part of the dialogue, but it is the mutual presentation through "correspondence" that lends life to them. When someone's words interest me, I am prompted to engage in an ongoing discussion. We might even become philosophical friends.

FRIENDS IN PHILOSOPHY

Does "philosophical friendship" exist at all? And if so, what does it mean? The history of literature and music shows famous examples of friendship, but do we know of similar relationships among philosophers? Some of them, like Hegel and Hölderlin or Hegel and Schelling, were friends for a while only, after which they became estranged. Is philosophy perhaps a way of life that makes friendship particularly difficult?

If philosophy were the solitary affair of uninvolved individuals whose mental eyes scrutinize the universe from a panoramic standpoint, one could still *share* such an attitude with one or more other lonely philosophers, but, even if these should come to the same conclusions, it would be difficult to find a special place for one's friend within the universe that unfolds before such an all-encompassing view. Doesn't a friend demand exceptional attention and devotion, which cannot be granted to most other persons? But if devotion (and thus towardness and facing) vanishes when it is thematized as part of a synthetic view, my friend and I do not meet *within* philosophy. Instead, we behave like hermits who get in touch only to borrow ideas for our private systems. In such cases, the stuff of which friendship is made does not lie within each one's solitary thinking; it must be motivated by some extraphilosophical interest.

However, the philosophy of a concrete philosopher runs counter to the panoramic overview of a freestanding observer, because it is always conditioned by the various commitments that have shaped the thinker's life and thought. Philosophers approach the common questions of their profession very differently, because their thinking cannot separate itself completely from the experiences that nourish it. True friendship certainly makes a difference for the way one conducts the experiment of one's life. If one's friend is also engaged in philosophy, both friends might appreciate each other precisely for their philosophical excellence.

Such a relationship can be analyzed with the help of Aristotle's classical distinction between the three main motivations of *philia*, if we may understand it as a distinction between simultaneously occurring motifs rather than as a distinction between three classes of friendship.[8] All friends seem to be driven by (1) some kind of excellence, (2) the usefulness of their relation, and (3) the pleasure of their intimacy. Friends appreciate each other's "being good at" something (for example, at courageously fighting or at skillfully making music), they want and expect mutual support and service (e.g., by lending money or by providing information about medieval philosophy), and they enjoy the (aesthetic, academic, gastronomic, religious, erotic, or other) pleasures of their companionship.[9]

Involved philosophers can become friends not only insofar as they enjoy *sharing* a particular tradition, a selection of favorite texts, a specific affinity with exemplary thinkers, or a devotion to the investigation of some questions they deem paramount but also because they have become attached to regular face-to-face discussions with other philosophers who have become partners of their thought-oriented lives. Some or many of their conversations might have a common goal, which is not restricted to private or public well-being. Within the historical community of philosophers, friends form small groups whose combination of personal intimacy with dedication to philosophical universality enables them to focus at the same time on one another and on the questions that each of them especially takes to heart.

A more elaborate study of such friendships would clarify their sociological and psychological relevance for the individuals involved and for the philosophical commonwealth as a whole. Philosophical friendship—or at least friendshiplike collegiality—seems necessary to concretize the abstract ideal of a dedicated search for truth. But what exactly differentiates its structure from the togetherness that characterizes the philosophical community as a whole? Friendships *particularize* the idea of a cooperative dedication to truth that is founded in shared desire, affinity, and sympathy. Friendly groups are better at close reading, truth-loving discussion, and mutual understanding than the all-encompassing republic of philosophy, in which there is so much competition, fear, blame, hostility, and misinformation, but insofar as friends are held together by the sharing of common interests and cooperation, they do not seem to differ from a well-disposed community of philosophers, except by their particularity.

However, if this is our conclusion, have we then not forgotten the direct, sympathetic, and very personal exchange through which friends offer their thoughts—and much more—to one another? Indeed, friends are bound together not merely by what they share (or by the being-with that constitutes them as a we) but primarily by addressing each other in proposing and responding. On the basis of a trusting relationship, they are involved in one another's search and struggle for the truth, without the distractions of political posturing. A philosophical friendship helps not only to prevent or overcome the constant threat of a narcissistic mode of thinking but also the danger of going with the flow of popular trends or running along the tracks of famous leaders. By speaking and listening to one another's approach to texts and questions, friends have an advantage in the conflict of interpretations that composes their milieu. But still—how much of their conversation is more than a particularization of the work that all philosophers have to do? Or should we reserve the word "conversation" for discussions among friends, while using it only as a euphemistic metaphor when we talk about philosophy in general? Obviously, the meaning of a word does not suffice to distinguish philosophical exchanges between friends from the dominant mores that concern all members of the philosophical community.

While listening to your speech or while reading your letter, I pay attention to the message that you transmit to me and make it a part of my thought. When you explain one of your insights, I follow the steps of your argument in order to see whether I can find them clear and convincing. I might propose an amendment or eagerly elaborate on your discovery, I may show that you are wrong or that you should check some fragile link of your argument, but in all such responses, I focus on the content of your speech—*what* you have written or said—while my reaction, though probably more benevolent than in some other discussions, must rigorously respect the standard code that rules the entire discipline. At the same time, however, I recognize in your words the characteristic voice and style in which much more than your doing philosophy is expressed. What you offer me is not a web of anonymous propositions, because several other aspects of your life—your mood and attitude, your struggling and hope, your perplexities and desires—echo in your discourse. My reaction cannot restrict itself to an abstract argument, because I hear your argument as only one—particularly revealing, but not isolated—aspect of your seeking truth, like and together with me. I am then with you in search of more than an abstracted or isolated philosophy. You and I are searching for more than propositions and arguments. We reach further—and this sets the tone for our conversation: in friendship we reach out to a philosophically cleansed and nourished life. As friends, we are demanding; what we want you and me to approach is philosophy as emerging from life itself and leading back to it. But such philosophy demands, on both sides, not only a symbiosis of thought and life but also a mutual understanding of your and my own progress in this respect. In other words, only philosophical friends are philosophical and friends enough to receive and return the other's words as existentially inspired and supported expression of seeking lives.

From the perspective of such friendship, we may venture to draw far-reaching consequences. For example, the following: even if you, my friend, offer me no more than a string of quotes, this would still be something special, because it is offered by you out of a friend's concern and in the unique mode of speaking that is yours. Like a fingerprint, the friend's voice cannot be mistaken for another's; the echoing of his or her unique life story makes all the difference for the concrete meanings of the address I hear.

Yet, someone could object that my recognition of my friend's voice does not *essentially* differ from the recognition of anyone else's voice, except that I enjoy hearing it differently. What then is so special in the philosophical words of my friend? Can this question be answered by a description of the features that single out my friend? Here we seem to meet with the old question of how we can know and define the singularity of individuals as individuals. If singularity is neither a lowest species nor an agglomeration of particular properties, how then can we form a concept of you or her as this singular person, thinker, and friend? Obviously, the perspective offered by Porphyry's tree is not appropriate to the way another's individuality reveals itself.

What or who is presented in speaking, insofar as it is not a general or particular form of speaking? Neither a beautiful or ugly voice nor an elegant or rigid style. Voice and style "color" and "shape" all speaking, but speaking itself—like facing, addressing, greeting, provoking, etc.—differs from all the possible qualifications it allows.

In some sense, speech, being more sourcelike and originary, precedes the modes of speaking it adopts to affect the listener. But even the expression I use here is inadequate, because it suggests that speaking (and addressing in general) fits the conceptual network that has been formed in order to capture essences, qualities, features, origins, and modes. Addressing and being addressed cannot find a place within the logic of such a categorical network. Your speaking, although always tied to something said, surprises me by coming from a dimension other than anything said or written and any context or interpretation. While speaking, the addressing presence of the author shows itself as simultaneously revealing and withdrawn. You, the speaker, are "behind," "before," or "beyond" the message that you offer to me. If the logic of essences, properties, and modes were universal and all-inclusive, speaking itself should be excluded from all logically justifiable language. If the semantic that corresponds to that logic has universal validity, then speaking as such must be called meaningless. If the saying is not a relevant component of anything spoken or said, however, it is nothing: nothing to be thought or talked about. But is another language possible to evoke and determine this "nothing," which constantly surprises and provokes all human beings from their birth to their death?

For once, we might attempt to explain *obscurum per obscurius* by drawing a parallel between the "nothingness" of God, as emphasized in negative theology, and the "nothingness" of you, this human speaker insofar as you talk to me. Because all attempts to identify God through essential and qualifying predicates fail, apophatic theology combats all idolatrous definitions by indefatigably negating all forms of positive predication about God.[10] Somewhat similarly, we must state that all attempts to qualify or define you who speak to me will fail because your speaking cannot be reduced to anything spoken of. Indeed, the impossibility of capturing God or a speaker in positive propositions has even deeper roots than the deficiency of a language that is tied to essences, properties, and modes, substances and accidents, grounds and effects. The mere fact of talking *about* God or *about* speaking makes both of them disappear. They present themselves only to an attitude of listening *to,* looking up *at,* opening oneself *toward*—an attitude of awakened attention, expectation, responsiveness, dedication, or devotion. Just as God withdraws from all language *about* God, so too the human speaking that affects us shields the speaker from any attempt to define him or her as an object or theme. Yet I obviously "perceive" you (who look at me and speak to me) insofar as I am affected, touched, surprised, and provoked by your words—though not so much by their content but primarily by their reaching out to me, however poor or empty their content might be. The reaction that your addressing me provokes in me is not in the first place some thought or talk about the truth or the worth of your message. Your turning toward me urges me to offer attention and possibly some words to you; i.e., you urge me to turn to you by a responsive address, in which I signal my personal and interested presence to you. Speaking changes the course of the listener's life by directing the listener's attention to the speaker and thus instigating some kind of devotion. By provoking me to a response, you commit me to a form of answering that contains the beginning of my responsibility for you. If you succeed in turning me around from my immersion in private affairs to being interested in you, you have converted me. True, your addressing me leaves me most often enough initiative to turn away from your appeal, thereby cutting the embryonic bond through which you make me co-responsible for a common future, but, as a refusal of your appeal to my responsiveness, such a cut implies violence. If my refusal stems from my being obsessed and possessed by solitary reflection, it shows that my philosophical ideal is a strictly private Cogito. But how then can I be a member of a larger community? And how could I ever become a philosophical friend? By thinking *about* everything, without paying attention to other thinkers who arise "behind" and "beyond" the sayings and writings through which they reach out to me, as one of the many for and to whom they speak or write, I isolate myself and try, for my part, to distance all others who approach me. However, what is more important: the fate of communicating thinkers ("the philosophical conversation") or their words as material for private meditation?

The answer to this last question depends upon our understanding of "importance." Should a philosopher maintain that Plato's work is important for philosophy (including both its historical and systematic dimensions) while maintaining that Plato himself does not matter? If this were the answer, the meaning of his philosophy can be separated from the meaning of the human life that—at least partially—expresses itself in it. Then, Plato's philosophy would obviously be far from an existential affair. Neither would similar philosophies continue the ancient and medieval project according to which "friendship" (*philia*) with "wisdom" (*sophia*) includes the acquaintance with and practice of a successful life.

If speaking is revealing, even apart from the message it conveys, its relevance involves the *unicity* of the speaker: you, who invite me to engage in a responsive relationship. My responding is, of course, another speaking (or writing or gesturing) through which I, whom you have made an addressee, become an addressor by presenting my unique presence to you, who provoked me. How can you and I be so similar yet absolutely unique at the same time? Through addressing each other as you, not me.

But what is so proper to philosophical friendship if the ongoing conversation between "you's" and "me's" is "essential" for the life and communication of the entire realm of philosophy? A first answer to this question might be that philosophical friends realize concretely the ideal "to and fro" between you and me that belongs to but is rarely emphasized within the worldwide network of the philosophical conversation.

However, if the unicity of the speakers cannot be captured by any description of specific features, if your speaking reveals a "nothingness" "beyond" or "before" all species, how then can speaking and listening, unicity and (cor)respondence be relevant for the emergence of friendship in philosophy? If we make an abstraction of all that can be thematized in order to concentrate on the speaking that allies friends, does this alliance then differ from the relationship that connects me to anybody else who demands my attention by greeting me or sending me a letter? *Everyone* who "speaks" to me confronts me with a unique—radically different and yet similar—destiny. In addressing me, all who face me—if only from their pictures in the newspaper—reveal to me why I cannot doubt their universal *and singular* right to exist. And not only their right. Deeper than and antecedent to their rights (which can be delineated within the framework of a system), their eyes speak, thereby making me responsive and responsible for their unique and irreplaceable destinies. If this is not an invitation to radical—and thus also universal—friendship, then what is?

Several metaphors have been proposed to indicate the community-forming element of the original, unchosen but demanding alliance that allows us to speak of one encompassing humanity. Especially "fraternity" and other familial metaphors have been used to indicate the pre- or supranational, metalingual, and supracultural commonality of all humans, a commonality that has been regularly denied by the historical arrogance of nations, cultures, and religions. Only a worldwide *philia* would be capable of relativizing all human divisions so as to realize the necessary conditions of peace. If friendly philosophizing only implied concentrated interest in the unique fates of a few speakers, would such a practice of philosophy then be truly wise or rather sectarian and esoteric instead?

Before we rush to any conclusion regarding the universal unicity of each actual or potential speaker, we need to be more enlightened about the unique nothingness that is revealed in their speaking. Because it does not belong to the dimension of the said, the "nothing" of your and my speaking coincides neither with human nature nor with any other essence. Several names have been proposed to signal how noble, admirable, and lovable the "almost nothing" is, which provokes us through its absolute claim from beyond the combination of pleasure, usefulness, and virtue that motivates an Aristotelian friendship. Kant called the person an "end in itself" and recognized that its absolute "dignity" (*Würde*) transcends all values (*Werte*). Perhaps he was too quick when he identified dignity as the source of all *moral* imperatives, for, as absolute, it surpasses the dimension of virtues and vices. Indeed, nobody can be identified with his or her moral standing. Moreover, until death, there is always hope for conversion, and we are not wise enough to judge the dead.

What then is the response that truly respects and does justice to the "nothing"-like (or absolute) dignity that lights up in the masks to which idolatrous interests reduce the innumerable faces that look at us? Not only attention, interest, respect, or awe but also assertion, assent, and consent, affective confirmation, saying amen, and blessing—a will to heed and foster the "almost nothing" of the absolute unicity that speaks universally, a "*volonté de promotion,*" as Maurice Nédoncelle put it in his unjustly forgotten *Vers une philosophie de l'amour et de la personne.*[11]

If we affirm that true friendship, as ultimately motivated by reverence for "speakers" as such, transcends all attachments to pleasure, utility, and virtue, we seem to stretch the meaning of friendship to its extreme limits. But what would then be the place and meaning of friendship in a more restricted sense?

Recognition of every singular human's unicity demands concretization, but this implies also particularization. Universal recognition of all individuals remains an all too abstract ideal, as long as it does not crystallize in communities and groups whose members realize it in particularized relationships, manners, and modes of action. Schiller's "Be embraced, [all of you] millions!" splendidly glorified in Beethoven's symphonic hymn to universal love, is too illusory and cheap as long as it does not become a concrete face-to-face of testable sympathy and singularized concern. Thus we can think of friendship as a universe of concentric circles, each of which have their own conceptual and affective tonality and style, and a characteristic degree of proximity and intensity, from the ultimate horizon of worldwide solidarity to the most intimate forms of partnership and love.

Particular religions, civilizations, cultures, nations, regions, professions, schools, and associations provide us with contextual conditions of concrete devotion. Sharing professional or existential interests with others generates affinities that may develop into close friendships. In philosophy, these can emerge when philosophers treat their questions as invitations to cooperate with others in the common search for truth.

Within such alliances, some may be struck by the admirable or lovable *manner* in which others are unique, not merely in the universal sense of speaking as such but also in the sense of their remarkable voice and style of philosophizing. Whether an encounter leads to lasting friendship is largely a question of fate. As gifts of grace, friendships are too contingent—too surprising, gracious, fortunate—to be deduced as a necessity or claimed as a right. Even affinity or convergence in philosophical work is not a sufficient reason for becoming friends in a more emphatic sense. However, if philosophy is the dimension in which we attempt to speak a language that transcends all particularizations without abolishing them, and if we do not want universality to degenerate into a totalitarian view of "masters and possessors,"[12] then philosophy is a privileged dimension for friendship on various scales. The practice of philosophy does not stop at becoming wiser *about* friendship, however. By practicing friendship within philosophy, one might become wise enough to pay a philosophical tribute to the unique lovability of each and all.

SIX

Vocative

You smiled at me; you uttered words to me; you addressed me. Me? The baby I was could not yet designate himself as a me or I. You awakened the slumbering I in me, who already answered your smiling, your talking, before I became aware of myself. By addressing me, you provoked me to reactions, which addressed you. You forced me to respond. My smiling answered your smiling.

You challenged and summoned me; you did not allow me to close you out by withdrawing into myself. You saved me from imprisonment in my skin. You freed me from solipsist slumber and isolation. In fact, I have never been *solus ipse* because, from the beginning, you and I were not only different, with separate destinies and destinations, but also linked forever.

Since my birth you can call me, because there is this distance that confronts me with you. You took the initiative for our exchange of looks, smiles, voices, words, and expectations connecting you to me and me to you. Your naming me, the first vocative that drew me out of my sleep, revealed to me how impossible it is to be alone. It introduced me to the real life.

How many times has some voice drawn me out of similar, including more sophisticated, slumbers: the many dreams that transformed all existences into hedonic elements of my private realm, where even you existed for my pleasure alone. If you had not been there to provoke me, I would not have become human, for I cannot listen, respond, call, address, provoke as long as I remain an asocial component of the universe.

Responding to your voice that calls me, hearing and not avoiding but attending to a vocative was the beginning of my becoming *me* as ego, *I*. In it began my regarding, meaning, speaking, intending, aiming, participating, accepting, willing. Responding gave me a direction.

Your addressing me makes me address you. Your call establishes me as an interlocutor; you enable me to take a second, responsive initiative. The vocative generates a nominative. I never am a first, originary, origin but always second, a latecomer. And you? You too were provoked to become a speaker by your parents, who addressed you in the language they inherited from theirs. Language has no beginning, although and because it cannot exist without being spoken by speakers who are thrown into it without getting a chance to choose or resist. The language into which we are born owes its existence to speakers whose language would not exist without earlier speakers who . . . , and so on.

As soon as I am able to speak or to write in my own name, I count on a series of explicit or implicit vocatives to reach an audience that, I hope, will listen to my words or read my inscriptions as directed to them. All words would remain fossils if they were not reanimated by voices that address them to others, who thereby become you for the speaker. The power of my invocation involves all individuals who pay attention to it in a basic—albeit embryonic and uncertain—form of alliance. Their names, John, Mary, Francis, Beatrice, or simply "you," are not unique, but each of my addressees is as unique and irreplaceable as I myself am; and we are connected by calls that must be answered.

Even if you refuse to listen to my vocative, your refusal is an answer, sometimes even a very eloquent one. The power of my allocution can be resisted, but it cannot be ignored or undone. At the same time, my addressing you makes me vulnerable. In greeting you, for example, I expose and display for you who I am and how I exist. I can attempt to mask my weaknesses or fake a better appearance than I deserve, but you might pierce the crust of these defenses, and I am, at least vaguely, aware of the difference between the truth about me and the figure I put up to charm or impress my interlocutor. In any case, however, the addressing itself cannot be performed and hidden at the same time.

In a phone call, one can hide many properties but not the calling itself; the directness of my targeting you is then particularly focused and intense because the listener is not distracted by other—visible, touchable, smellable—modes of self-presentation. True, by skillful acting I can modulate the tone and rhythm of my voice, but the degree of my (in)sincerity can be heard by a sensitive ear. I can try to make myself absent while addressing you. By writing a letter, for example, or sending a tape, I can avoid being vulnerably displayed when you read my letter or listen to my tape, but even then, you (re)imagine my presence with or without the masks I might have used to be favorably different from my clumsy or poor reality. Moreover, it is possible that I have changed since I wrote my letter to you and that you are addressed by a writer who belongs to the past. To a certain extent, this is always true when time prohibits the speaker from coinciding with vocatives and messages that are received at a later moment.

When I try to make myself absent in my speaking, I open a distance between the self-presentation that is contained in my utterances and the person I here and now, still and already, am. This distance easily leads to lying and insincerity, but these can be heard. Acting, to be a good or bad actor or actress, can be forgiven, even enjoyed, if its fictional character is obvious, but what does it mean that the vocatives in a play are calling without exposing any real I? Even the addressing can be faked, but a fictive address cannot be understood without reference to an authentic one.

To expose myself as I really am—e.g., as vulnerable or not so good, nice or learned as I would like to be—demands humility, because I then must love the truth more than faked authenticity. It demands also courage and patience, because I must risk and endure that you discover the deficiencies behind my charm or diplomacy. On the other hand, greeting you might expose not only bad but also some good features of which I myself am not well aware. To know myself, I might need a conversation with someone who is a better judge, even if she is puzzled by her own degree of goodness and authenticity or their contraries. The truth about me seems to need someone other than me to be impartial, free, not bent by my biases, not contaminated by my betrayals and perversions—even if that other may be contaminated by many other or the same weaknesses and self-betrayals. The symbol of the all-seeing eye expresses the idea of a perfectly sincere, authentic, and true judgment that would confront my wishful thinking about myself with the person I really am. Don't I need—and don't I *desire*—such a confrontation in order to know whether and to what extent I am respectable—perhaps even lovable—for someone who loves the truth? Can anyone deny that we desire to be loved? But do we desire to be loved *in truth*? Do we irresistibly hope that some powerful kind of benevolence will recognize our lovability *despite* its (partial) corruption? Do we count on the possibility of forgiving and compassion? But even then we do not want to be tricked by our masks and faking.

The many voices that reach us through calls, allocutions, letters, cards, texts, books, inscriptions, and so on inform us about a host of situations, events, relations, thoughts, and experiences, but they cannot reach us unless an implicit or explicit vocative assures their destination. What motivates those voices? To whom are they directed? Do they want to reach me?

Ancestors and classics need intermediary voices that redirect their words and texts to reach you and me, who live later or far away, but no word can draw our attention—it cannot be heard or read—unless someone, who thereby becomes (a) you, offers it to us. Before we can understand or study any information, we are recipients: open to and—at least somewhat—interested in considering the message that is sent to us. Your vocative draws my attention; it wants to seduce me to attentive listening or reading. If the voice is ignored, the speaker is saddened; it is bereft of its proper meaning by falling on deaf ears.

Seduction is not successful unless it satisfies or awakens an interest in the listener. A message would never concern me if I were not interested in it at the moment it reaches me. We are interested in many messages, especially we, who spend most of our time deciphering, analyzing, interpreting, and writing texts and commentaries. Our interests are expressed in paraphrasing, explaining, reconstructing messages, and producing new ones that continue and transform the traditions in which we are at home.

We offer our own talks and papers to new recipients, who again contribute to the history of words. However, what kind of message is conveyed by our vocatives?

In the texts we study, explicit vocatives are not numerous. Even letters of Paul or Augustine, Goethe, or Hölderlin are studied because of the religious, philosophical, literary, psychological, or historical information we may find in them, but the addressing voice as such and the receptive addressee are rarely thematized during our hermeneutic operations. The factors, the situations, the psychological and cultural differences that determine the transmitted meaning of the *messages* are clarified, but we rarely concentrate on the addressing act by which a message becomes a gift and establishes a bond. When focusing on the contents of our texts, we silence or neglect the vocatives that bring them to our attention. We are not even able to hear them as long as we are fascinated by the information that is provided by the texts.

What is the meaning of a vocative as such? What does it do? What does it add to the information conveyed and addressed by it?

If, for example, an explicit vocative is used in a philosophical or theological dialogue, the use of a name or "you" invites someone to consider a topic *about* which one can tell or think a lot of things. That all considering, telling, and speaking *about* is also a telling and speaking *to*—even if I speak only to myself—is often forgotten but always presupposed. The presentation by a vocative intention is taken for granted, but what sort of intention is here at stake?

When you address me while pronouncing my name or by simply calling me "you," perhaps accompanying it by a meaningful gesture or look, you put me in the perspective of a recipient who either turns to you or away from you. If I do not turn away, I respond to your call by listening. By targeting me, you then make me the center of a new situation, which you originated, while at the same time orienting me toward you, who, from your perspective, also remains central, even if you behave in a quite humble way. Both speaker and listener are central, but they take turns in initiating and responding. If I receive your appeal and pay attention to it, I show thereby that I am interested in what you have to say, but what is your interest in addressing me?

Your and my reciprocal interest in each other can be motivated by a shared interest in specific kinds of information. For example, we might be curious about your health or well-being. Or we communicate about findings of your and my philosophical research. Or you summon me to justify my managerial decisions in a department of our company. What do all such interests concerning work, functions, research, or health have to do with the vocative that accompanies our exchange of words about them?

When I hear you introducing a conversation by addressing me as "Adriaan" or "you," you might want to focus on my functioning or otherwise being part of some business or system, without being interested in any other aspect of my being this person to whom you turn your attention. The vocative through which you single me out then names only a certain aspect or figure of me—neither the entirety of my existence nor its most fundamental core. Yet, I might feel flattered and to a certain extent recognized, because your naming me liberates me from being a completely anonymous component of a human mass, in which no particular individual—and certainly no unique singularity—is perceived. If, for example, you quote a sentence of mine in one of your publications, I might see this as a sign of recognition on the level of scholarship. But I do not want to be reduced to being (only) a scholar. In the act of addressing me, the use of my name targets and touches a person who has more properties than scholarship, although, from a semantic perspective, neither "Adriaan" nor "you" as such signifies, expresses, or summarizes that "more."

In a sense, the vocative does not contain any information; it only *addresses*. Meant and heard as addressing me—i.e., as sent by you and accepted by me (in the first-person position) as coming from you, who thereby turn to me—the vocative establishes a bond. It not only indicates or designates me; it also recognizes and engages me as somehow interesting and worthy of the caller's—your—attention. This attention can be motivated by your interest in the value of my function, work, or utility, which then still restricts the interesting aspect of my personality to its "economic" dimensions, but even so your calling me cannot entirely ignore or erase the underlying and basic fact of my undeniable, unrepeatable, irreplaceable, and unique existence.

Although my unique existence as such, in all its abstract barrenness, cannot exist without the particular and individual features, products, functions, relations, and situations into which it has unfolded and will unfold, it can be meant and recognized as such. My existence, as the *hypokeimenon* that "precedes" all its operations, cannot be excluded altogether, even if you want to evaluate me from an exclusively functional or economic standpoint, for the unfolding of my existence into its worldly and social—and thus also economic—realization is not separated from it by an abyss. However, some uses and experiences of the vocative concern so intensely the core of your or my own existence as such that all the rest becomes irrelevant.

What kind of experience is expressed in a vocative that concentrates on someone's existence as such alone? It is addressed to someone as a simple affirmation or appreciative confirmation of the addressee's very existence as distinct but not separate from its concrete unfolding in an adventurous and historical life, which has its negative and positive, its happy and unhappy, its good and bad sides and events. The intention that ensouls such a vocative ("John!" "Mary!" "Angel!" "Honey!") approves the existence of the one who is named, whatever great or tiny, splendid or disgusting, useful or destructive actions or works this person achieved or will be achieving. It recognizes and blesses the unique and absolute worth of the addressee, without taking into account what he or she may have produced or performed. And since it wills and says "amen" to this person's existence without being motivated by any other property than her or his unique human existence as such, the addresser must be able to transcend all economic, scholarly, esthetic, political, financial, and even moral exigencies. To pronounce such a vocative consequently implies that one is able to look away from all good and bad properties and productions in order to concentrate on this person's unique existence. This includes the ability and willingness to condone and forgive. In other words, this vocative can do without any addition by informative sentences. It is self-sufficient: the pronunciation of the name expresses love. Mothers, fathers, lovers need this vocative to communicate without being distracted from the core of the beloved's existence by any other business and their involvement in it.

To be perfect, it is not necessary for such a call to know how beautiful or helpful or good the beloved really is, because that is not the basic and ultimate question. Existence as human and unique is here at stake, but what this is and how one responds perfectly to it, is, in the end, a secret.

First of all, however, it is a wonderful fact wonderfully experienced in a love that is called "disinterested" because it discards all other interests than the lover's basic and supreme interest in the beloved's unique existence as such. Whatever adventures and works your history unfolds, you are lovable because you are human and unique.

The secret does not disappear, but it is illuminated when we realize that you—in your uniqueness—are preceded by an absolutely archaic vocative, which called you to existence. By confirming and blessing your being while it unfolds, that kind of voice continues the amazing initiative of a gratuitous creation, which stretches out over your and all times of human emergence and dying. If the originary Word is creative ("God spoke . . . : the light was"), its form must be an incessant vocative: a voice that inaugurates and lovingly confirms, sustains, orients, accompanies, and guides each one's unrepeatable but dissimilarly similar destiny. Faith in the Creator then means that we hear in each human existence the perdurable welcoming by which it is blessed.

If hell exists, it must be the horror of no longer being able to respond to this fundamental welcome. But heaven has already started for those who are enabled to enjoy the Speaker's call and join it by multiplying its benevolence toward the never identical promises of all who happen to exist, thanks to the absolute affirmation—the original *Jasagen*—of the Voice that inaugurates all speaking by a preexistent vocation that grants future without end.

SEVEN

Philosophy versus Faith?

For Giovanni Ferretti

If philosophy is a way of life,[1] the lives philosophers live—before, during, and after becoming philosophers—are relevant for the orientation and the content of their philosophies. Although much of a philosopher's personal and historical past can be forgotten, transformed, or rejected in a philosophy that emerges from it, that past cannot entirely be ignored or left behind. Consequently, the question of *how* a philosophical thought is, can, or should be rooted in a philosopher's factual existence cannot be fully answered by universally valid statements about philosophy's point of departure and method—neither before nor after the heyday and death of existentialism.

To initiate the following meditation on the relations between the lives of singular philosophers and the philosophies that emerge from such lives, I would like to begin with two rhetorical questions, which, perhaps, have not always been taken seriously enough in methodologies of philosophy: How could students be initiated into the practice of philosophy, if their teachers could not appeal at once to (1) their own extensive education, during which they have learned how to live, experience, and reflect; and to (2) a similar, but also different, education that has formed their students? How could a teacher and a student communicate with each other if both of them do not share a certain level of acquaintance with human existence and cultural assumptions?

If competence in philosophy could be acquired in complete independence of prephilosophical experiences, beliefs, convictions, customs, and modes of expression, one could imagine that the study of philosophy can or even must begin with a tabula rasa. This fantasy, though, has never been realized, and it seems an impossible condition. All the philosophers we know of have come to philosophy as already knowledgeable about many persons, relations, things, and events. They were trained in one or a few of the six thousand existing languages; their knowledge was marked by a particular culture and their behavior by the mores of their surrounding. Before they became acquainted with philosophy, they had learned enough to be capable of living and speaking in a more or less sensible and reasonable way. Like their lives and thoughts, our living and thinking have been led by a certain form of *phronesis,* which together with other factors has motivated our decision to study philosophy. We remain marked by a historical past, a shared language, the input of particular educators and traditions, the mores of a specific epoch, and by a host of personal and interpersonal, affective, practical, and cognitive adventures. Dedication to philosophy has certainly changed our lives, but have our skillful deductions completely replaced or swallowed up what we have learned from life itself? Many facts can be gathered about the changes that certain philosophies have caused in the lives of philosophers and the influence of their lifestyles on their thought. In this chapter, however, I will focus only on two leading powers of thought and life and ask to what extent they influence or even determine the philosophy that emerges from the thinker's life. Provisionally, one can indicate those powers by using the traditional pair of reason and faith, but in order to set the stage where they meet, some additional remarks about the interaction between philosophy and life seem useful.

Between osmosis ("a philosopher's entire life is markedly philosophical in all its dimensions") and separation ("consider your philosophy a business that must be performed from nine to five, after which you can enjoy your real life"), there are other more realistic varieties of a philosopher's existence. But the core question aims at discovering (1) whether there is something in each human life—or perhaps only in singular lives—that spontaneously reaches out to a particular kind of philosophical reflection and (2) what, in philosophy, is necessarily bound to certain prephilosophical elements of a human life.

During the last hundred years, the conception of philosophy as "a way of life" has been rediscovered. Was this rediscovery a symptom of profound dissatisfaction with the modern ideal, according to which philosophers would have to develop universally valid theories in the name of a generally shared reason and evidence alone? But how could the recognition of the indispensable role that particular and personal characteristics play—not only in human practices but also in human thought—coexist with the demand that philosophy should be dedicated to the production of a universally valid theory? If philosophy is indeed a way of life, how then should we understand the relations between existential acquaintance and philosophical knowledge?

Since reason has been the central power in the history of modern philosophy, it is hardly possible to answer this question without a preliminary reminder about the contrast between reason's qualifications, as seen by the main trends of the philosophy in which most of us have been educated, on the one hand, and the role reason does and should play according to those who see the intimate links of reason with other modes of contact and acquaintance as unbreakable, when they plead for a more existentially inspired philosophy. Let us therefore begin with a brief sketch of the philosophical program that, from Descartes to Hegel, has dominated the professional practice of thinking and even now survives in many introductions to philosophy. Instead of attempting here an adequate reconstruction of the origins and history of modern philosophy,[2] an outline must suffice. I apologize for its overly schematic and simplistic character but hope that it is acceptable as a foil for the contrasts that I want to emphasize.

THE MODERN PROJECT AND ITS DEMISE

The modern emancipation of philosophy from political and religious ideologies implied a strong confidence—Hegel even called it a "faith"[3]—in the autonomy of human reason. Reason was proclaimed the ruling power of human nature, given to all individuals who are mentally healthy, well educated, and mature enough to participate in sensible practices and conversations about earthly realities. Using their senses and guided by reason, normal persons can discover the truths they need to make sense of their existence within the universe. We do not need a Church or Academy—and even less the State's political authorities—to tell us the truth; we ourselves can find it through the mobilization of our natural capabilities. To terminate the endless fights between insufficiently proven opinions and theories, it is necessary that we begin anew, from scratch, without relying on any of the present or past authorities (including the dominant traditions). History is not important; existing faiths and biased forms of education are certainly facts of life, which are taken for granted in everyday existence, but in philosophy we bracket them, because there they lack validity as long as reason has not demonstrated them to be true. As philosophers, we begin with a clean slate. In contrast to all pseudo-philosophers, who try to justify unproved convictions, dogmas, or ideologies, we only accept rational and empirical data and principles that are so obvious that they resist all possible doubts.

Over time, the historical search for self-evident data and principles has turned out to be more difficult and controversial than expected. The determination of a pure, wholly uncontaminated beginning—the true beginning of all future philosophy—developed into an obsession with (the only adequate) *method,* while unstoppable discussions in the precincts of philosophy led to many splits in rationalist, empiricist, idealist, positivist, pragmatist, and skeptical directions. Descartes, Spinoza and Leibniz, Locke, Berkeley and Hume, Kant, Fichte and Hegel announced their methodical discoveries as if they finally had discovered the right approach, but their ongoing self-corrections prefigured the endless debates that still continue within a more and more formalistic realm of epistemological and metaphilosophical considerations and reconsiderations.

Continual disappointments are the result, but more audacious, though often less precise, attempts at renewing philosophy by returning to concrete—existential, social, and historical—experiences and experiments have become louder and more numerous. After Pascal, Rousseau, Hamann, and Herder, a range of post-Hegelians like Feuerbach, Kierkegaard, Marx, Nietzsche, and Bergson succeeded one another in brilliantly proposing different venues, but none of them can be seen as the founder of a unified community whose members agree on a new mission or method. Only Husserl, who explicitly referred to Descartes, seemed to succeed in being followed by some kind of movement or school, but even his new beginning was quickly diversified, corrected, transformed, or replaced by his sympathizers. During the century that followed Husserl's attempt at founding a new hegemony, many divergences have again shattered the hope that now, finally, all philosophers could have a clear idea of the true or best philosophical approach and, more specifically, of the role that reason and experience—including the experiments and the adventure of life itself should play in our performance of philosophy. Again the basic tenants of a new methodology have exploded, like the former attempts at unification, thus again generating multiple heresies. Some of these heresies appeal to *hermeneutics* to justify their dependence on various pre- or nonphilosophical elements, neither quite obvious nor entirely proved, of the past or present. More or less plausible beliefs, convictions, customs, symbolisms, stories, poems, myths, and epochal affinities are again admitted as supportive or illustrative elements within the boundaries of a widened conception of philosophy. Together with several philosophical and extraphilosophical authorities from whom we continue to borrow, we are rediscovering the importance of our cultural and religious history as a source for philosophy. Appeals to Plato, Aristotle, Plotinus, Hobbes, Kant, or Hegel are not rare, and individual autonomy seems to take a back seat when, for example in ethics, the authorities of Aristotle and Kant are invoked without excuses for borrowing from both. Medieval authors are less welcome, however, because many thinkers of our epoch do not feel at home in their frameworks. The pervasive presence of God and faith in medieval philosophy is certainly one of the factors that displease those thinkers who have decided that "metaphysics" and "ontotheology" belong to an irretrievable past. Regrettably, however, their decision is rarely supported by a thorough discussion of the meaning of the word "metaphysics" or a serious reconstruction of the ontotheological tradition as it has developed through almost all the great philosophers from Parmenides to Hegel.

PHILOSOPHY AND FAITH

Medieval philosophy seems to be an undigested past of contemporary philosophy. Although a splendid renaissance of scholarly studies on Christian thinkers from Clemens to Cusanus is going on, rarely are their insights creatively retrieved in new philosophies of our epoch. Platonic and Aristotelian but also Cynical, Stoic, and Epicurean elements are used more often in retrievals of philosophy's past than are medieval insights or arguments. If, indeed, our epoch is post-Christian, one can understand that retrievals of ancient Greeks are more frequent than reappropriations from Augustine or Scotus, but should it also mean that we no longer can learn from the philosophical conquests that were performed within an explicitly Christian framework? If numerous philosophers of our epoch do not hesitate to (re)actualize pre-, post-, extra-, and anti-Christian beliefs, why exactly would they despise the wealth of medieval thought or consider them outdated?

In the Western hemisphere, a lingering mistrust accompanies the thought of a "Christian philosophy." Much more than "scientific philosophy," "feminist philosophy," or "Anglo-Saxon philosophy," the expression "Christian philosophy" almost automatically raises the suspicion that such a "philosophy" can only be biased. It must be contaminated by authoritarian beliefs whose validity should be carefully checked before they can be admitted to the domain of autonomous thought. Since hermeneutics and appeals to widely accepted opinions and beliefs or to impressive poets, scientists, and other nonreligious authorities have made so much progress, one would expect that an affinity with the Christian tradition no longer would be considered an impediment for performing authentic philosophy. However, adherence to a specifically Christian perspective has remained more suspect for secular—really or "only methodically" atheist—philosophers than an Anglo-Saxon or French bias. But why should only secular, areligious, or Godless thinkers constitute the forum that sets the rules for authenticity in philosophy?

If such a forum were the high court of philosophy, it would necessarily declare or assume that religion must be excluded from philosophy unless religion can justify its contributions as philosophically relevant for the philosophical discipline, whose rules and presuppositions it must obey. Could religion then still have a proper meaning by itself? Should it be appreciated but also classified as an imperfect version of the truth, which is captured more adequately by philosophy? Or should it be unmasked as a sublimated presentation of something other than the truth?

We are no longer so naïve as to deny that many biases, obsessions, and impure attachments can hide behind religious beliefs and practices. As a critical and self-critical discipline, philosophy must proceed with suspicion concerning all theories and practices that are presented without strong credentials or plausible arguments for their claims. Since Empedocles and Parmenides, the best traditions of philosophy (like those of religion) have insisted on the many distorting biases that may hide behind ideas and ideals that are produced by our desires and drives. Consequently, they have emphasized the need for self-critique, purification, and catharsis. But the question of impurity or contamination is different from the question of whether any authentic philosophy should be universally valid and universally recognizable as such.

No philosopher, however secular, religious, sober, down to earth, or mystical, is a blank soul without particular affinities and attachments. Our philosophical conscience seems to demand that we make ourselves absolutely independent with regard to all preferences and assumptions—even the most ingrained and commonly accepted ones. Only this would give us the right to judge in philosophy. But is it humanly possible to be and act as entirely reduced to, and one with, the wholly unprejudiced purity of reason alone? Would not such a condition—to be nothing other than reason itself—imply that one is already wise? If a philosopher is required to produce an absolutely autonomous and unprejudiced philosophy, such wisdom would be a condition for the correct beginning of all philosophy, not the end or ideal (or illusion). If, however, the philosophical *eschaton* lies in a wisdom that embraces the entirety of a philosopher's life, it asks more, not less, than the operations of an autonomous reason alone, for then the philosophical self-critique of our own thinking (including its beginnings) cannot be separated from an existential self-critique of the life from which that thinking emerges.

But let's concede that the question of God and religion cannot be compared to the question of how French or Anglo-Saxon a philosophy is allowed to be and focus instead on a more restricted question: "Can the philosophical community trust persons whose religious faith is at least as deeply rooted as—and perhaps even deeper than—their full and sincere dedication to philosophy?"

This question sounds different within the horizon of a hermeneutical philosophy than it sounds in an "enlightened" world, where the participants believe in the possibility of an uncontaminated autarky of genuine philosophy. Within hermeneutics, one is aware of the grown but neither wholly proved nor immediately given elements of all philosophy, including its Greek, Roman, Jewish, Arabic, modern, enlightened, romantic, postmodern, secular, pagan, feminist, German, French, British, North American, South American, African, Southeast Asian, and other versions.

Since Descartes' program for a fully autonomous philosophy finished in exhaustion and disappointment, enough historical studies have been published to enlighten us about the neither evident nor demonstrated assumptions, opinions, beliefs, and deep convictions—many of them inherited from the scholastics—that guided Descartes himself and his successors, including, for example, Leibniz, Spinoza,

Wolff, Kant, and Hegel. Post-Hegelian philosophers have recognized, with more grace than their eighteenth-century predecessors, that philosophy cannot begin without explicit or implicit recourse to certain sub- or prephilosophical assumptions that are not only philosophically relevant but also determinant. Among them, *faith* stands out as the main contender over against the claims of an autarchic—and in this sense completely unprejudiced and autonomous—reason.

A philosophical investigation of the relations that distinguish and link faith and reason, as they present themselves at this moment of history, demands a host of precisions and an overview of the numerous analyses that have been proposed during the last century. I cannot give such an overview here.[4] Instead, I can try to focus on one meaning of faith, the one that seems to be the most relevant for our discussion of the bonds that unite philosophy and human life, while postponing a more elaborate investigation of the wider field that reaches from superficial kinds of opinion and belief to the most profound meaning of faith. This approach cannot do without situating the selected phenomenon of faith vis-à-vis other phenomena that might seem similar to it, as suggested by names like "belief," "conviction," "trust," "loyalty," etc., but even such a task demands much more than one or two chapters can accomplish. Here, I will restrict myself to an evocation of that faith, which is the most fundamental motivation that grants a person or a community its basic stance and dynamism.

DOXA, ETHOS, FAITH

As born into a determinate family and educated in line with the convictions and customs of a particular subculture, each of us shares a cluster of opinions and practices with many others. The ethos we thus inherit and appropriate can be analyzed according to all the affective, practical, imaginative, epistemic, aesthetic, ethical, and religious dimensions and layers of human existence. Participation in a dominant ethos shapes each one's basic attunement to the particular environment and the singular events, processes, and traditions of a shared but also individual history. A multitude of spontaneous, hardly examined or critically tested beliefs and practices characterize us insofar as we share a common ethos, including a more or less coherent pattern of perceiving and interpreting the—spatially and historically rather restricted—world that has become the general pattern of our adjustment to the given place and time that we did not choose but have to live in. Large parts of the scene in which we live our lives—for the most part in conformity with the mores of our milieu—sustain and condition our speaking and acting without necessarily prompting us to radical forms of questioning and critique. When distance toward our own existence awakens us to reflection, we are already set in ways of living and thinking that have largely become obvious, "natural," unproblematic, or even automatic and immutable.

Self-examination can begin in philosophy, but there are other ways that lead to knowledge and critique of self and world. Philosophical scrutiny is certainly an excellent mode of identifying and critically testing the "obviously correct" practices and convictions that have become our own. While dedicating our intellectual energy to a philosophical revision of the existential singularity each one of us has become through the turns and returns of a strictly personal history, we discover that it is neither easy to acquire an insight into the genesis of one's own way of life nor to justify it by philosophically coherent means. Many of the conditions that made me such as I have become remain obscure—and the same is true of the shared conditions that characterize our community and the epoch in which we live. Often we must guess why I did this and not that, reacted in a particular way to some unexpected event or took an unpredictable path when nothing seemed to urge me to do it, and so on.

Epics, dramas, novels, history—sacred and profane—can help us to understand the great variety of motivations that play a role in the twists and turns of a human life, but beyond all questions regarding actions and reactions, surprising events, and particular motivations, we discover that each person's course is driven, energized, pushed forward, led, and oriented by a basic and primordial passion from behind and before all the particular conditions of one's character: a will or desire that longs for a meaning that justifies my existence by making it worthwhile to be lived. What gives me a direction, movement, and further evolving stance is the core and kernel or the secret of what I—most profoundly—am. This discovery does not lift the obscurity by which that secret is enshrouded. The secret does not—and presumably will never—show itself in the form of a transparent concept. It cannot be formulated in one or more sentences or compared to any thing, person, entity, or occurrence, but it determines all that is relevant for the conduct, the quality, the meaning, the encompassing hope, and the central love of someone's existence. It is not only an origin or source of a life's proper meaning—and thus the beginning and principle of all beginnings and principles—for it permeates and inspires or co-inspires all the affections, desires, motivations, and insights that unfold a person's capabilities.

The deepest and originary recognition of this secret origin can be called *faith,* if this word is taken in its most decisive and existentially relevant meaning. And that which is intended by this faith is the one hidden but all-surpassing, all-inspiring, and all-orienting longed-for beyond all the affections, thoughts, and motivations that spring from it. Many call it "God," while trying to clarify its abyssal, absolute, and infinite difference from all ends and idols, gods, and "Gods." Others might prefer to leave it nameless or call it by other names, such as the Absolute, the Ultimate, the One, the Sought. Self-professed atheists identify their longing differently, for instance as the most originary pathos of life itself or as a basic trust in Nature, the Universe, Humanity, or History. They may find their basic motivations in sincere dedication to humanity, the poor, justice, the Good, or Beauty itself as source and totality of all generosity and illumination. But all who are awakened to the irresistible Drive that both singularizes and unites all of us have entered a dimension—the most basic one—that we can call *religious,* if "religion" may be used in its widest, preconfessional, and preparticular sense. Plato's pointing at the Good in his *Politeia* or to the "Beautiful itself in itself" in his *Symposium* and Plotinus's reduction of all being and thought to "the One" belong to that dimension. Whether and to what extent religion, in this very wide sense, is universal, so that it can create a deep affinity between all "positive" religions, including the Jewish, Christian, Muslim, Hindu, and Buddhist ones, is a difficult question that will not be answered here. From a modern-philosophical standpoint, one might be tempted to see all religions as specifications of a universal genus, which has been called "natural" to indicate that it naturally springs from the human *natura* or *essentia,* but this fact leaves the question open of whether philosophy possesses the best or the highest perspective for answering the question just asked.

While pursuing our examination of the relations between faith and philosophy, I will restrict my focus to Christianity and begin by asking how Christian faith and philosophy relate to each other insofar as each of them characterizes the lives of persons and communities that are marked by both.

From the perspective of philosophy in its typically modern version, briefly sketched above, we can enumerate the following characteristics of those relations. The philosopher adopts a panoramic perspective, because only such an all-encompassing viewpoint permits the philosopher's mind to inspect freely its object: the universe, which includes not only nature and history but also all the good and bad prejudices that might beset the human mind. Universality and totality but also coherence and conceptual unification are essential for such a freestanding position, which must produce a universally valid and thus a supraindividual theory.

All the religious practices, principles, prayers, and prejudices are part of the universe thus displayed and investigated. The elements of truth to be found in them must be translated from their religious expression into a philosophical—i.e., systematic and conceptual—language. Whereas the philosophical perspective must remain neutral with regard to any particular position, the various positions represented in religion appear before the universal forum of a universally valid reason that transcends all singular and particular perspectives. In philosophy, only the human mind, as ruled by reason, has the right of the last word about truth. Individual philosophers are only translators and messengers of a universal *logos,* which speaks through them. What, in their work, is not or not yet quite true belongs to their singularity or to restricted agreements among like-minded individuals.

Hegel's system is perhaps the best example of all the Western attempts to realize the modern ideal, but he spoke in the name of many others when he demanded his students to empty their minds from all prejudices except their "faith in Reason."[5] In his mind, Philosophy surpasses a merely formal—*logical* and *methodical*—recourse to reason. As rooted in a pre- or suprarational faith, it had to be celebrated as the power through which the absolute Spirit, religiously known as God, governs the human mind. Faith in Reason thus became a faith that not only competed with but also surpassed the Christian religion, which Hegel saw as the summit and completion of all other religions. According to his interpretation, this faith expresses the fully true truth of perfect philosophy in an affective and imaginative but not yet fully rational, i.e., conceptual, mode.

Could modern philosophy have been saved from developing into a faith? Can it still realize the presumed innocence of an entirely unbiased viewpoint, or is philosophy's stance inevitably pretentious and arrogant?

In the name of many faiths—Jewish, Christian, Muslim, even Buddhist, Hindu, and Shinto—numerous forms of terror have been perpetrated, and faith in reason is not an exception. During the French Revolution, a Temple of Reason was built for a new liturgy according to a new calendar: the most visible adherents of the former faith were murdered to make place for the blessings of a new era. The schema has been repeated many times by other revolutions that were named somewhat differently—scientific, dialectical, social, democratic, and so on—but we can shove them aside insofar as they represented only bad imitations or idolatrous heresies of the philosophical ideal they invoked to justify their brand of philosophy. If we can make abstraction from all such misunderstandings, can we then save the idea of a completely rational philosophy as characteristic of the best of all intelligent faiths and consequently as fundamental and pure enough to offer the basic justification of a fully human way of life?

Before answering this question, we must focus more sharply on the relation between Christian faith and philosophy in its double possibility of being (a) a merely formal—logical and methodological—discipline, generated by reason, and/or (b) a faith in reason that treats all other faiths as rivals, whose differences in competency in the end must be judged by philosophy alone.

If philosophy is practiced as a faith in the basic and strong sense sketched above, it is wholly committed to its own perspective, which it considers the highest and all-encompassing one in the realm of truth. It then must see all other attempts at reaching basic and all-encompassing truth as competitors, whose claims and results it must refute or integrate. If, however, philosophy considers Christian faith to be only a kind of defective theory, it will mobilize its own empirical, logical, and methodical criteria in order to evaluate the form and content of the Christian doctrine, as if this were no more than another attempt at rational explanation of the phenomena, comparable to the philosophical attempts. The philosopher will then ask to what extent the Christian vision is rationally justified or lacking in well-established principles, correct arguments, and demonstrated conclusions.

Insofar as philosophers have been able to show that certain historical configurations of Christian faith contained irrational, antirational, or unreasonable elements, Christians owe gratitude to them for their help in detecting elements that cannot be proved on the basis of elements that are philosophically admissible. However, regarding those elements of the Christian tradition that are neither immediately given nor found philosophically provable, philosophy cannot draw final conclusions if it cannot give convincing arguments why one should consider it to be the supreme judge in questions of truth. To give up this position presupposes, however, that a non-, meta-, or suprarational faith is not necessarily antirational and condemnable but possibly better than a philosophically justifiable position. If the revelations to which Christians appeal grant the faithful a higher perspective with other criteria than philosophy, and if, consequently, the philosophical perspective must be subordinated to a *meta*philosophical faith, we must test the potential of that higher perspective. If such a perspective opens up in a fully authentic and pure core of the Christian faith (and/or in other religions' faith), then the philosophical faith in Reason is no longer the uncontested judge of all judges. It has then been unmasked as one of the many faiths that compete for the first place among the most pure and authentic and encompassing accesses to the truth. Just as the Christian faith, the philosophical faith in Reason has then become debatable and subject to suspicions from the side of those who have reasons to see it as contaminated by distortions, hidden biases, hubris, superficiality, lack of passion or sincerity, idolatry, or narcissism.

Christian faith, i.e., faith in God as revealed in Jesus Christ, is primarily neither a belief—not even a most basic or foundational belief that underlies all other beliefs—nor a philosophy, if philosophy is a freestanding, neutral, and autonomous investigation of all beliefs or noetic systems. It is not even equivalent to a theology, because it is first of all the dominant energy and inspiration of a life that is turned, in hope and love, to the Absolute. Consequently, neither this faith itself nor its "object" can be captured in a proposition, a sentence, a concept, a syllogism, or a theory. Its quintessence implies the pathos that drives all humans toward the secret that we, while borrowing from Platonic and Christian expressions, may call the Sought,[6] which, even before it is found or known, is already loved. Before preachers, theologians, or philosophers explain that God exists and what, who, or how God is, faith intends and relates to God as the greatest, deepest, and most decisive but utterly mysterious presence, whose infinite lovability is protected against all curiosity and arrogance by being profoundly hidden and ineffable.

Instead of believing *that* God is or exists as such or so, the core of faith lies in the *commitment* that engages and involves the faithful in a direct relation of being addressed by God and addressing the Addressee in response to God's overwhelming lovability. The encounter with God is somewhat comparable to a face-to-face relationship that stretches me when I look up to a human person who loves me. Since

God is infinite, however, faith and love toward God encompass the universe of all that exists, and especially all humans, including our own affective, practical, and noetic economy. In faith, one does not primarily respond to the call by speaking or writing *about* it but rather by turning *toward* the caller in a commitment that is made of acceptance, gratitude, dedication, and devotion. Faith thus mobilizes and orients the entirety of one's existence from top to bottom—affectively, practically, and noetically—toward the creative source of all that can be encountered and celebrated but also—though secondarily—admired and contemplated. But God cannot be investigated or explained—not only because God is not given as a describable phenomenon but primarily because the beloved cannot be studied from a distance, as long as the lover is involved in loving the beloved. Insofar as theology imitates or borrows parts from a scientific or philosophical methodology, it cannot give an account of the giving mystery, on which it would like to fix its exploration, because the explicative distance needed for its studious perspective withholds and flattens the transcending rush of its devotion.

However holy or sacred theology tries to be, the dogmas it produces cannot do full justice to the ineffable Origin if they are not tightly integrated as internal moments of clarifications within the erotic relationship with the addressing addresser. How often has it already been said that modern theology has been fatally wounded by its divorce from spirituality! But do we have a clear answer to the question of how exactly we may overcome this separation by *reintegrating* all theoretically orthodox explanations into the loving faith of a grateful, hopeful, pious, and honestly edifying speaking to the Origin of all speech? Do we know how to practice philosophy in a spirit of prayer and devotion?

At this point, we meet again with the question of how we are able and allowed to speak *about* the Beloved without betraying or weakening the thrust of talking *to* the One who awakens and orients our love. In other words: How can we unite our prayers with a studious form of contemplation? Or how can we integrate our learned sophistication into an attitude that looks up in adoration? Statements, dogmas, and treatises that have been tested by ages of speaking about God create distance rather than intimacy, but they can remind us of what, in the end and from the outset, is at stake. Praise and adoration are better approaches to the Ineffable than philosophical or theological expertise. Whoever denies this prefers theory over faith and liturgy.

EIGHT

The Universality of a Christian Philosophy

Two central questions that I will engage in this chapter are: (1) To what extent is philosophy necessarily universal? And (2) does the philosophy of those who belong to the worldwide community of Christians (the *Catholica*) distinguish itself in this respect? Beginning with some remarks about the universality of philosophy, I must then also consider the relationship between philosophy and faith, and I will do this by focusing especially on its Christian versions. I will argue (1) that Christian philosophers are necessarily influenced by their faith and (2) that the authenticity of Christian philosophers is not endangered by their faith commitment.

UNIVERSALITY

The universality of philosophy can be approached from various angles, such as its *subject matter* (what are the material and the formal objects of philosophy?), its *claim* (are its statements universally valid?), its *audience* (to whom should philosophers speak?), the *thinker* (from which stance and in the name of whom does a philosopher speak?), its *method* (must a philosopher be guided by experiences, principles, and a logic that are available and acceptable to all people?), its *language* (in which language—Greek, Latin, German, English, French, Italian, Chinese, or other—must a philosopher speak or write?), and the *soil* from which it emerges.

It is not difficult to add several other angles of approach, such as the *context* in space and time, the *expectations* a philosophy raises, the *limits* it cannot surpass, and so on. However, I will not try to be complete in my attention to certain aspects and conditions that may be responsible for the extent to which philosophy is universal or not. But *faith* deserves special attention, because it has such a profound impact on the entire life of the faithful, including those who dedicate themselves to the praxis of thought. Is faith an impediment or an incentive, or is it indifferent with regard to the universality of an authentic philosophy?

THE SUBJECT MATTER OF PHILOSOPHY

Western philosophy emerged from amazement about the cosmos as composed of parts and elements in amazing connections and movements. Parmenides and Heraklitos tried to understand how all things (*ta panta*) form one whole (*to pan*) while being related to one unifying principle (e.g., *einai,* the *logos, Moira,* movement, *polemos, to hen*) that also differentiates them. Throughout its history, philosophy has maintained this all-encompassing character. Clear examples are to be found in the programs and systems that were presented by modern thinkers from Descartes and Spinoza to Fichte and Hegel, but even postmoderns who insist on the fragmentation and differential pulverization of human thought continue to extend their thinking to the ultimate horizon of the universe in which we live. True, the claims of philosophy have never included all the details of the universe—in fact, they have become even more modest since abandoning many issues to the sciences—yet philosophy continues to search for the all-encompassing and basic principles and the ultimate limits of all that is. The universal and unifying character of philosophy seems to belong to its essence.

PHILOSOPHY'S CLAIM

Philosophy claims to speak the truth when it states its theses as valid for all human individuals and communities. History, hermeneutics, and cultural relativism have shaken our confidence in our ability to capture universally valid truths, but we still teach and publish our findings as worthy of being known by anybody who can read, and we still try to convince students and colleagues that at least some of our statements are valid for everyone. If we are doubtful about certain theses or if we accept amendments, we implicitly agree that our convictions are judged by the truth itself, whose verdicts should be accepted by all who genuinely seek the truth.

Perhaps we are more intensely aware than past generations that all philosophies are conditioned by inherited, communitarian, cultural, and personal biases, but even so we cannot stop considering them to be biases with regard to the unbiased truth, which keeps us searching for it. We consider all those biases to be particular and partial—albeit bent or contaminated—modes of access to the one genuine and overall truth, which gathers its friends through affinities that connect their theoretical approaches. Such a view is justified if we may postulate that the truth itself hides in a variety of versions and disguises. We do not abandon the hope that even the best disguises can somehow familiarize us with the blinding generosity of the never plainly given yet powerfully attractive truth itself. If this presupposition is acceptable, our best method might be to adjust and amend, further explore, and radicalize the most promising of the paths with which we are acquainted, in order to clarify at least some aspects or outgrowths of the truth. Such a wager might provide us with a better guidance than an entirely new search for initial agreement or the distillation of an abstract principle from the different approaches, for such a commonality is too thin and inconsequential to be interesting, whereas the thorough renewal of a particular path that has proven to be worthwhile stands a better chance of advancing toward the hidden truth than do the more easy and mediocre agreements of the average thought and experience.

The wager that is proposed here has consequences for the philosophies of Greek and Roman, Jewish and Muslim, Christian and post-Christian thinkers, but before we focus on the relations between philosophy on the one hand and religious faith on the other, let us consider the other aspects of philosophical universality.

THE AUDIENCE

What modern thinkers from Descartes and Hobbes to Hegel wrote was and still is read by a restricted community of educated people. However, the universal validity of their discoveries was seen as a criterion for the quality of their writing. Philosophers naturally thought of themselves as addressing all human individuals who desire and seek the unifying truth. When national languages began to replace the traditional Latin—at a time when the explorers of the earth and history in their immense diversity of cultures began to discover humanity as a whole—the philosophical pluralism became, more than ever, a serious problem. In the meantime, "philosophy" has become the name for a scattered "multiversum" whose unity remains an open question. Besides being greeted by promotions of American, British, French, German, Italian, African, Indian, Chinese, and Japanese philosophies, we are confronted with many basic and methodological differences. Will we be seduced to join one of the many—empirical, idealist, pragmatic, analytic, scientific, existential, or phenomenological—brands? It no longer surprises us that philosophy, in spite of its claim to universal validity, can be characterized by such a diversity of perspectives and horizons of interpretation. But how are all those distinctions meant? Do they indicate confinements and exclusions? Who is forced or invited to listen to the representatives of all those different approaches? And, to single out a special group, who are the philosophers that call themselves Christian? How do they practice philosophy, and to which audience do they direct their thought? If they do not want to abandon the conception of philosophy as addressing itself to *all* who are interested in thinking as a way to universally valid truth, how then can they, at the same time, call their brand Christian? What does this characterization mean? If Christianity constitutes their own privileged background and that of their audience, will this be obvious from the style and content of their papers? If so, is this aspect of their philosophy then not detrimental for their claim to be philosophers—and not masked theologians? Perhaps some of them—especially the Catholics—are ashamed of representing a Church that, for centuries, not only has caused so many political, cultural, and sexual scandals but also for centuries has resisted and fought great advances in science, law, governance, exegesis, philosophy, and theology. In response to those scandals, some Catholic philosophers avoid speaking about a "Catholic" or a "Christian philosophy" while insisting on their loyalty to the worldwide republic of un- or otherwise-believing philosophers, whereas others struggle for a balanced position with regard to their double participation in the "enlightened" civilization of the West, on one side, and the tradition of Christian faith, on the other.

These and similar questions are intimately connected with questions that arise from the next three aspects of philosophy listed above: the *thinker*, the *method*, and the *language* in which philosophy is done. Taking all the listed aspects together seems to be a minimal condition for acquiring some insight into the relations between the Christian *faith* of certain philosophers and the philosophical *universality* that is supposed to transcend the barriers dividing different schools and styles.

THE PHILOSOPHICAL SUBJECT

Regarding the thinking subject, modern philosophy offers several theories that are based on the autonomy of reason and experience. In the most famous monuments of modernity, the original "I think" is declared to be independent from all political, religious, ideological, and other authorities, whereas much of the postmodern literature treats the Christian faith as an outsider of the philosophical culture. It has been replaced by a widespread celebration of a self-conscious freedom. Theology may use what philosophy discovers, but the latter can see religion and faith only as puzzling phenomena that demand empirically and rationally testable explanations. In any case, the methods of science and philosophy of religion must themselves be faithless.

At the same time, however, philosophy itself has discovered that the Cartesian project of philosophical autarky was either utopian or too abstract to generate real truth. The formal—logical and methodological—conquests that have been accomplished do not provide a sufficient description of any concrete thinker. The geographical, historical, linguistic, cultural, characterological, and biographical character and situation of the thinking subject are recognized as inherent to the perspective that conditions and colors the thought that emerges from it. Some postmodernists have reduced the philosopher to a combination of empirical and categorical, partly conscious and partly subconscious determinations, while attempting to show that philosophical operations, like all other ideologies, are derivative from factors that cannot be controlled or changed by thought or willful interference. Consequently, philosophy is then interpreted as the expression of a stance for which no thinker can take full responsibility. Defenders of the subject have answered that the alleged determinations are only suggestive conditions that leave the various thinkers free to transform them into elements of original—and rational—constructions. However, most adherents of both parties have maintained the modern principle of philosophy's radical independence from faith or theology. They share and enjoy the conviction that authentic philosophy is free from all religious interference.

Many Christians share the conviction that philosophy must be completely independent in order to be loyal and faithful to its own principles alone. This conviction founds their indignation toward any suggestion that their own philosophy, despite their demonstrations and assurances, is recognizably Christian. This indignation might even be greater if someone confronts them by defending the general thesis that no thinking—whether Christian, Jewish, Muslim, atheist, deist or agnostic—can be separated from a basic faith in which the thinker's life is rooted, because it consciously or unconsciously cannot avoid borrowing from such faith or from adjusting to its implications. Or, to put it otherwise: *every human individual not only lives but also thinks from out of a basic faith, and no philosopher is able to adopt an Archimedean, wholly neutral, and faithless standpoint.*

Strictly autonomous thought, in the strong, wholly independent, and autarkic sense of this word, demands such an Archimedean perspective, because it needs enough distance from the natural and cultural universe of which the thinker's own life is not only a part but rather the ownmost, inescapable perspective and thus the center of experience and reflection. To find a freestanding perspective from which one can think of oneself as an uninvolved and wholly unbiased eye (i.e., a transcendental—and thus universal—I), one should be capable of excluding not only all deficient but also all particular perspectives, preferences, perceptions, affinities, languages, and cultures from interference. In order to communicate philosophically with all other humans, one should abstract from all differences in gender, age, epoch, habits, signs, symbols, and personal contingencies in luck and disaster. Once stripped down to the nakedness of a genderless, silent, neither singular nor particular, undistinguished representative of humanity as such, one would have to be neither a he nor a she, nor a you nor I, because only that would make us free from all natural, civilized, historical, and personal character and biases. What would such a transcendent ego see, feel, imagine, or understand? What could it share with all other individuals? In any case, it would not be a person who, thanks to traditions and education, has integrated a particular language, culture, taste, style, or specific kind of communication. If it were possible to mentally bracket all nonuniversal properties so that a completely naked transcendentality emerges from the real me who wants to reach the anonymous summit of nonparticularity, however, I would not be able to really live and think without immediately reincarnating that naked skeleton in the highly contingent, incorporated, and acculturated body of my singularized particularity. If this concrete I, with its own characteristics, happens to be deeply rooted in a basic faith, such incarnation naturally encompasses not only that transcendental skeleton but all the elements that are unified, animated, inspired, and oriented by that permeating faith. A loyal thinker—loyal to both his religious and his philosophical convictions—necessarily tries to transform the allegedly neutral and anonymously universal elements of thought that come to his or her mind into integrated parts of a faith-based thought. Of course, it is possible—and at times realized—that some faithful thinker does not or cannot integrate her philosophical thoughts into her faith-inspired convictions but instead juxtaposes them, because those thoughts do not easily fit into the horizon of her faith. But such an unmastered juxtaposition, without even a bridge between philosophy and faith, creates a tension that urgently demands some sort of unification. For philosophy wants consistency, including at least some understanding of the connections between, on the one hand, the basic and ultimate horizon of the philosopher's mind and, on the other, all that this mind shares with those who practice philosophy, even if they are characterized by different prephilosophical assumptions and other horizons. Before I give an argument for the thesis I just formulated, however, I would like to premise it with some remarks about the *method(s)* and the *language(s)* of philosophy.

METHOD

The history of modern philosophy shows a remarkable concern for the establishment of the right method. Even before the most encompassing thought takes its departure, we must already know how we should proceed to capture the truth about the reality we are going to investigate.

The natural sciences and mathematics have played a paradigmatic role, because they showed how many participants can agree on a set of clear principles and rules that guarantee success and agreement in discovery and explanation. However, the history of modern methodology has also shown a strong diversification and a growing awareness that metaphilosophical and even metamethodological reflection itself must again and again struggle with the same problems as prior, more naïve and straightforward philosophies. In the first place, an autonomous philosopher struggles with questions like "How shall we begin?" "Which one(s) of our self-aware, implicit or still hidden assumptions may we take for granted, and how must we proceed before we have successfully finished our preparatory search for a valid method?"

Descartes' attempt to determine, once and for all, the only correct method, has had to be redone time and again, and each time a characteristic procedure—whether rationalist, empiricist, idealist, historicist, vitalist, psychoanalytic, structuralist, or other—was proposed as the one that finally would terminate the search for a suitable beginning. While many philosophers became more and more involved in *formal* questions, structures, and conditions without end, they and many others postponed or forgot the main questions of *content*, including the most interesting ones—such as those concerning beauty, goodness, love, and the meaning of human lives and communities, or they left such questions to common sense, because they were too difficult and controversial. Many kinds of belief and trust survived the learned considerations of meta- and meta-meta-philosophers, whose distance from human life-as-it-is-lived grew, whereas their mutual agreement about vital questions of life and meaning did not. On the contrary: the scene of Western philosophy exploded into a multiplicity of schools, streams, groups, more or less original views, and epigonal clubs.

To what extent can philosophy today be considered universal? Do the philosophers still form a community? Can philosophy still be defined in some more or less univocal or analogical sense of the word? If not, within which generally accepted framework could such a definition then be proposed? Don't we need a philosophical superphilosophy to give an insight into the (real? possible? partial? impossible?) unity of existing philosophies? Or must we, like Descartes, begin with a clean slate in order to stipulate, declare, construct, decide, vote, impose, or pray for one philosophy that we promise to accept as the only one that from now on must be universally recognized as the universally valid one?

Even that will be impossible if philosophy remains at the same time a passion *and* rooted in a deeper than merely philosophical conviction, trust, or faith. For then, not only other existential and communal but also philosophical phenomena and interests are necessarily influenced by the philosopher's deepest—and to this extent prephilosophical—conviction, trust, or faith.

LANGUAGES

If Greek were *the* language of philosophy—as the slogan goes—genuine philosophy would have died long ago, at least since the death of the last philosopher for whom ancient (but post-Homeric) Greek was a living language. However, philosophy has survived by learning Latin, Hebrew, Arabic, Italian, Spanish, French, German, English, Dutch, Portuguese, Russian, Polish, and many other languages. After the twentieth-century wave of veneration for "language" sometimes bordering on idolatry, it no longer seems necessary to emphasize the huge influence a particular language has on the tone, structure, shape, climate, coherence, rhythm, and style of philosophical thought and writing. The kinship of philosophy with rhetorical, literary, historical, musical, mathematical, and other forms of eloquence has again become apparent. With regard to the relations between philosophy and faith, the links between scholarly, kerygmatic, liturgical, rhetorical, poetic, and narrative forms of language deserve renewed study, but here it may suffice to focus only on the fact that philosophy must speak in one of the many particular languages, even if it may, or sometimes must, borrow the idiom of other less well-known languages.

Since philosophy is inevitably polyglot, it lacks a literal universality. True, to a certain extent, it can overcome this lack by encouraging translations, but we know how even the most accurate and faithful translations are only approximations of the original. We also realize that even the reading of texts in their original language does not allow a reader to think the very thoughts of the original author, but this does not prevent us from continuing the conversation, even with ancient and medieval thinkers. Although we do not have a proof of it, we trust that a certain form of translatability—and thus an approximative universality—is always possible, whereas we at the same time know that neither Greek, nor Latin, nor French, nor British or

American English can pretend to be the universal language of humanity. Consequently, the truth of a universally valid thought can only approximately be expressed in *any* language. Or, should we again believe that one of the many languages is the unique one in which truth itself speaks or writes? Mustn't we conclude that the full and universal validity of the pure, not yet particularized truth keeps silence while hiding behind, or in, a variety of lingual versions? Truth, though, seems to be a seducer: it prompts us to approximative discourses in a host of competing languages. Each of these languages has its own manner of mediating, but the universal truth itself remains silent, granting us only prismatically diversified manifestations.

THE SOIL OF PHILOSOPHY

Culture and history, in their entanglement, form the soil or the bedrock—or whatever metaphor one prefers—from which philosophies emerge. Even those philosophies that more than others resist the wear and tear of time must be reformulated, revitalized, and retrieved in order to inspire those who live in other contexts than the ones in which they were generated. They die forever, if they are not transformed by new, re-creative thinkers. But great thoughts always seem to find such rethinking heirs, even after they have been forgotten for centuries or buried in epigonal rehashings.

After the successes of hermeneutical theories and practices during the last two centuries, we no longer have to insist on the necessity of creative repetition, but aversion toward epigonic imitations and scholastic repetitions of already existing -isms, on the one hand, together with ongoing reverence for originality, on the other, have conspired in neglecting an important aspect that is equally obvious in the study of the cultural and epochal contexts from which new philosophies emerge: their being bound to certain traditions that are not—at least not explicitly—philosophical.

The last two centuries certainly have taught us the art of tracking down implicit quotations, influences, borrowings, references, and more or less original retrievals, but most often, the specialists of this art have confined their work to links between past philosophies and later ones. The history of philosophy has excelled in genealogies that did not exceed the boundaries of philosophy itself (including the theoretical regions immediately surrounding it). Without diminishing our gratitude toward the great scholarship of those specialists, we must recognize that a much more difficult task is still waiting for equally excellent accomplishments: the study of the not explicitly philosophical factors that have codetermined the various philosophies and their conflicts. Within the horizon of the present chapter, we especially would like to know to what extent and how Christian philosophers today are marked by their education and the conduct of their daily life within the double environment of Christian faith and secularity. As Christians, they cannot feel in complete agreement with the dominant standards of a secularized society, but even as a minority, they cannot step out of it. In the worst situations, the practice and theory of their faith is reduced to a private affair without impact on their public life, but can a philosophy remain completely private? If it can or must, what sort of political, moral, cultural, religious, and historical philosophy would bloom within the limits of such privacy? Could one trust philosophers who leave their deepest convictions at home in order to publicly conform to the dominant ethos of a pagan or idolatrous State? Who can then still be sincere? Must we withdraw from politics and liturgy to hide in catacombs? This would exclude us from the congregation of those who, like Hegel, are convinced that there is no truth, except "in" (or as) "the whole." For, which whole, unless the eschatological one, is then still inhabitable? Should we, in discussion with utterly secular friends, mute the most radical and decisive part of our convictions regarding the meaning of human life, the universe, and history? Or must we concede that the deepest convictions do not have anything to do with an authentic and public philosophy?

But what about the basic convictions of our secular interlocutors, if these conform to the average culture and ruling ethos of our time? Some, or perhaps most, of them claim that they do not appeal to any particular faith or fundamental trust. They are just decent members of a modern, enlightened, more or less liberal and conservative, free, egalitarian, and democratic society. If they rely on any trust, it might be a combination of common sense, scientific observation, logic, reason, individual freedom, human rights, and democracy. If these form the soil from which autonomous philosophies grow, however, no thinking philosopher can avoid asking how such a trust can be justified—or, at least, recommended—*philosophically*. Even Hegel recognized that the decision to embrace Reason (*Vernunft*) as the Alpha and Omega of philosophy was an act of faith: "To begin with, I cannot demand anything else than that you bring along trust in *Wissenschaft*, faith in reason (*Glauben an die Vernunft*), trust and faith in yourself: the courage of truth, faith in the power of the spirit, is the primary condition of philosophical study."[1] Any philosopher, not only a Christian one, will respond to this proclamation by asking (1) how credible it is, (2) how it can be the beginning of an autonomous *Wissenschaft*, and (3) how it differs from the various forms of religious faith into which millions and millions of nonphilosophers *and philosophers* have put their primary and deepest faith and trust.

THINKING FROM OUT OF FAITH

Let me now try to develop an argument for the thesis already stated above: There is no Archimedean (or transcendent) standpoint from which one can think about the universe (including all the natural and cultural differences that distinguish the thinker from other humans). Or, in a more positive vein: the thinking of a thinker who is rooted and at home in some kind of faith is inevitably influenced by this faith and must give an account of the mutual relation in which he or she thus is involved. If we are able to prove this thesis, the next question will be whether the reflexive account can be a philosophical one or whether it necessarily refers the thinker to theological considerations.

Although a full demonstration of this thesis demands more argumentation than I can give here, I aim at showing that it represents a reasonable position, which not only reconnects with the premodern

Greek and early Christian conception of *philosophia*[2] but also liberates the thinking of Catholic thinkers from some self-imposed restrictions that might derail their thought into an anti-Christian form of philosophy. To realize this purpose, we must briefly consider some tenets of a basic metaphilosophy and, for reasons that will become clear in the course of the following sketch, we must anticipate some theological aspects of the issue at stake.

A *first* step, which does not yet focus directly on faith, would characterize philosophy as a combination of experience and logic in the broadest sense of the word "logic," i.e., as encompassing all appropriate uses of attentive and rigorous thought. Although it is often forgotten, it is clear as day that both *experience* and *thought,* however naturally they may be given, also must be *learned.* Such learning includes a process of maturing and purification. Neither are immediately given as perfectly accurate and uncontaminated organs for apprehending reality as it is. The most trivial facts, such as "this is a pencil" or "there is a cat on the mat," might be obvious to everyone who understands English, but they have little or no meaning if they are isolated from the complicated context of the concrete and contingent features and the existentially different circumstances to which they explicitly or implicitly refer. No philosopher would care for such truths if they could not be shown to be relevant details of a particular constellation that challenges particular and singularized responses through thought and action. Neither isolated propositions nor entire theories seriously interest any philosopher if their relevance for the human life of specific persons in historically concrete circumstances is ignored. Ultimate questions are especially interesting because they deeply affect people, including thinkers, who are explicitly motivated by the search for meaning. If philosophy is more than a noncommittal game, it is a logically stylized thematization of the experiential and phronetic elements of genuinely lived ways of existence. The adventure of an individual life is supported by a characteristic stance, while its movement is guided by illuminating and puzzling experiences, amazing discoveries, regrettable mistakes, painful conversions, and enjoyable renewals. As an important part of human life, philosophy likewise is and remains rooted in existential positions, while its movement—through education, growth, and katharsis—is guided by an experience of life-bound thinking, which involves us in more than logic and observation, toward the kind of wisdom it needs.

A complete analysis of the process through which a thinker becomes genuine and wise would show the fundamental roles of affectivity and imagination in this process. Blindness to these roles has frequently been justified by the remark that feelings are merely "subjective." Feelings are indeed as "subjective" as thoughts and the most rigorous scientific theories, because none of them would even exist if no subject was involved in them, and *all* kinds of contact with reality can be biased, distorted, or mistaken, but if our emotions and thoughts are well trained and purified, both kinds of subject-involving activities are indispensable for getting us in touch with being as it is. That at least certain affections are relevant for thinking is implied by the old truths that philosophy emerges out of *amazement,* that the experience of beauty implies *awe,* that philosophy is impossible if not driven by *eros,* and that nothing is interesting enough to cause us all the difficulties of doing philosophy if it does not correspond to a *passion* for the truth. Of course, such intuitions cannot replace a systematic investigation of the relations between affectivity, experience, and thought, but they might be heard as an invitation to finally see such an investigation as one of the most urgent tasks in philosophy. It would present us with an updated version (enriched by psychoanalytical and anthropological findings) of the philosophical education presented in Plato's *Politeia.* In order to become a true philosopher (not a fake one, like the sophists), one must first become a *mousikos*: well formed, balanced, and tasteful in matters of feeling, passion, poetry, drama, and music. Only then will you have acquired the affective maturity that directs thinking toward the truth.

Having indicated this huge task, I hasten to the *second* step of my argument. If philosophy is an integral part of a lived life, it will be more important the more it is fundamental. Because a human life is a risky adventure that cannot be accomplished without an overall *orientation,* a leading *path,* a trustworthy position or *stance,* and an ongoing *move-*

ment of self-transformation, the philosophical search for truth plays an essential role in the development of its existential dynamism. The dynamism itself, however, is inspired by a still much deeper source or principle than emotions, music, logic, interpretation, or theory, namely by a certain *faith.*

"Faith," in this fundamental yet not necessarily confessional sense, is not the same as belief; it lies deeper than any opinion, belief, vision, or doctrine, because it is the grounding or rooting that precedes all beliefs, desires, passions, actions, representations, and systems in which it is expressed without being overtly exhibited. As the stabilizing, inspiring, encouraging, and orienting nucleus of a living person, together with his or her attachment to a certain community and the wide horizon of earth, humanity, and history, faith is the most radical trust that precedes and orients a person's desires, will, and reason. Because of its depth, it is much more hidden than explicit knowledge and reasoned behavior. Therefore, it cannot show itself "objectively," as if it were an observable thing or relation that fits the categories of our understanding. However, faith is not an inexorable fate or fixed necessity. On the contrary, it is the most radical and decisive response through which a unique individual reacts to the givenness of his own and others' existence in the here and now of this given universe. Each one of us is carried and driven by a basic trust, which places us on a primordial basis and adjusts us to an ultimate horizon. Philosophers are not excluded from this necessity; none of their thoughts or decisions can uproot them from the deepest of their "convictions," unless they pass through a radical transformation. Certainly, philosophy can play a role in certain changes of one's deepest faith, but such a conversion will then also change the philosophy of the involved thinker.

Instead of "conviction," the word "faith" seems preferable, because what is at stake is too deep to be captured by any doxa, article, axiom, or dogma. *Compared to faith, all theory is grey, and all belief secondary.* Faith is passionately lived, enigmatically embraced, and vaguely experienced rather than clearly perceived or emotionally transparent. Its character is closer to our originary and all-embracing affectedness than it is to self-conscious insights, motivations, decisions, feelings, or moods.

Its temporality is experienced as the present solidarity of gratitude and hope; while embracing the given—imperfect, but hopefully reconciled—past that continues to condition a desirously provoked future, we accept our failures with their erasure and bless the present as a mixture of expectation and unavoidable suffering.[3]

The *third* step of my argument follows from the difference-in-union between faith and philosophy in a single person. If philosophical thought is open to the entire universe, it ought not and *cannot* avoid reflecting upon the connections that link its own activity to the depth of faith and to the feelings, actions, and thoughts in which that faith expresses itself. If a thinker's faith is wholly or partly identical with the purest Christian faith, and if we may define *theology* as a faith-based reflection directed at clarification of the relations between God and humanity (while using all the necessary skills, including those of the best philosophers), the *philosophically* justifiable elements of that reflection are *ipso facto* parts or rather aspects of a *theological* reflection. If it is true that thinking is rooted in and oriented by faith, the thought of a Christian cannot be fully identical with that of a thinker whose basic stance and movement are different. Being the fundamental and ultimate dimension, faith—or, more generally, "religion"—has an effect on the entirety of a human life and on all of its relevant parts and aspects. This may not be readily apparent in all of its details, but it shows in the decisive issues and events where the ultimate meaning of a human life is most obvious.

Christians who practice philosophy cannot refrain from either explicitly or implicitly showing that their faith is more fundamental than their own and others' philosophical thoughts. To be saved, one does not need philosophy; philosophical ignorance is no obstacle for union with God. But how, then, is it possible that such philosophers at the same time aim at fundamental and ultimate truth *and* accept the imperative that reason *in philosophy* should be autonomous, or—to put it in a quasi-descriptive language—how can they restrict philosophy to the rational production by a faith-ignoring reason that combines its own universally valid principles with universally accessible and unbiased experiences?

Here I return to the thesis announced above. If faith, as basic stance and ultimate orientation, precedes, orients, inspires, and supports our experience of life and the movements of our rational reflection, then *autonomous philosophy is an abstraction.* The meaning of such an abstraction cannot be separated from the concrete life from which it emerges, although one can communicate with all other philosophers about the formal and experiential *elements* they also might recognize as valid, despite their different faiths. In the name of universality, philosophy can be practiced and defined as a discipline in which we speak a restricted language while hoping that we might establish a universally shareable level of agreement, but such a philosophy remains abstract insofar as it shies away from the most important and ultimately necessary questions concerning the meaning of human lives.

Within the totality of a faith-oriented *and* thoughtful existence, we must distinguish two dimensions: the most fundamental dimension of faith and the less fundamental dimension of universal thought. The "autonomy" of philosophy appears then to be abstract and relative; its universality cannot be isolated as a separate doctrine but only indicated as a shared element in all philosophies that come close to the truth. Philosophy exists only as inextricably entangled with a faith-inspired human life that searches for wisdom and conclusive meaning. A similar relation between faith and philosophy exists in the works of philosophers who are inspired by non-Christian faiths, even if they do not use the terms "faith" or "religion" to identify themselves.

One of the questions a philosopher asks is where exactly the border runs between the two dimensions of faith and universal (or quasi-universal) philosophy. If genuine faith permeates the entirety of a human life, it can neither be separated nor sharply delineated from the other existential dimensions. But then we are not able to determine the point or line where faith (or revelation) stops and ("natural") reason begins.[4]

When the earliest Christian philosophers adopted certain elements of ancient philosophy (such as statements about the soul's immortality and the existence of an ultimate Source or Cause), some of them interpreted these elements as products of the "natural" *logos* that belongs to human nature as such. To justify their interpretation, those Christians had to purify these elements from incompatible elements expressed in Greek mythology or Hellenistic world visions. But how were those Christian thinkers able to know that the borrowed parts were provable by the autonomous reason of a "pure" human "nature"? Have Christians themselves produced such autonomous proofs in the meantime? If so, are their proofs or quasi-proofs successful in convincing all humans, including agnostic or anti-Christian philosophers, or do they only convince people who already believe in their conclusions? Where can we find a neutral definition or description of "human nature," "natural intellect," "autonomous reason," and "faithless philosophy," in order to discover infallible criteria for distinguishing the difference between faith and reason or theology and philosophy? If Christians live in grace, and if their virtues, as well as their thinking, are influenced by the Spirit of Christ, are they then able to bracket that part of their intellectual endeavors that stems from grace, in order to know what their own and others' "nature" is able to prove in isolation from any prerational stance or influence or primordial desire? If "all is grace," where then are the limits of thought insofar as it is or is not permeated by grace?

At this point, many more questions arise concerning the autonomy of the logical and metalogical axioms of science and philosophy, the empty formalism of much contemporary philosophy, the boredom generated by its repetitiousness, its skepticism with regard to meaningful and ultimate issues, or—to be brief—the exhaustion of a tradition in which humanity proclaimed itself capable of conceptually recreating the entire universe. Obviously, one cannot handle the network of all these questions in one or two chapters. But let us at least pay some attention to a theological counterpart of the philosophical outline I just presented.

A THEOLOGICAL PERSPECTIVE ON PHILOSOPHY

The reach and relevance of philosophy is not only an issue for philosophy itself, which, in our days, often takes the form of a metaphilosophy, but also for a theology of revelation and human knowledge. As an essential element of the Western civilization, philosophy shares in the incarnatory and sacramental character of all spiritualization. Indeed, if divine Incarnation implies a radical transformation of human nature, the philosophical mode of seeking God participates in a thearchic search for ultimate union. To what extent have historically developed forms of philosophy in fact revealed certain aspects of God's truth—albeit in approximate and deficient forms? This question has been amply debated in early and medieval Christianity, and it remains an important issue not only within theology but also in any serious dialogue of Christian with non-Christian intellectuals. Here, however, I will restrict my attention to the human intellect insofar as it attempts to discover the truth by means of its own capacities alone.

As *created,* human freedom is called to well-being and well-doing regarding the existing universe, in which its own existence is involved. Born to be concerned, humans are primarily free to obey the unchosen demands of their (native) responsibility. Our initiatives and the adventures we dare to face, the conquests and discoveries we achieve, and all of the procedures through which we demonstrate our creatural kind of freedom are secondary to a responsibility that precedes our desire for being or becoming leaders of nature and history. Such leadership implies cooperation with the providential course of nature, civilization, and history, but the utopian fantasy of a demiurgical recreation that would make us "masters and possessors" of the universe seems a vain protest against our lack of absolute sovereignty. Similarly, the idea of an autarkic and all-embracing de- and reconstruction by way of conceptual reflection, characteristic of modern philosophy, contradicts the creatural dependence of Christian (but also Jewish and Muslim) faith. This faith recognizes that self-thinking, -planning, -ruling, and -deciding are glorious summits of human freedom, but it gratefully receives them as embedded in more humble attitudes. A metaphilosophical theology would have to show how a rooted form of a certain degree of autonomy is compatible with a devotion that intimately associates free thinkers with their gracious Creator.

A theology of human history cannot isolate creation from *sin* and *redemption.* The philosophical praxis of Christians and non-Christians alike participates not only in a general contamination of human intelligence but also in a divine healing whose traces are found among all nations. We need *grace* to overcome the attraction of arrogance and egotism. Responding to grace replaces a Godless faith in human autarky with a more receptive disposition toward the suggestions of a long and sacred tradition in which humans can feel at home, despite the fact that they are not able to deduce and perform some kind of salvation on the basis of self-certified principles. Faithful trust relativizes the "autonomy" of "natural" thought by integrating its *abstract* and *provisional* results into a synthesis of the thinkers' thoughts with the soil in which their life and those thoughts are or can be rooted. Only such a union opens the dimension in which the thinkers can think genuinely about the ultimate meaning of their philosophical investigations. As long as they stick to the provisional thoughts that present themselves when they restrict their attention to the domain of conceptual autarky, they are not yet thinking what they most truly are and already desire to be.

These hints are meant to prepare a theological interpretation of the manner in which philosophy should be practiced within the comprehensive whole of a faithful existence. The perspective of a Christian philosopher cannot entirely coincide with that of someone who, explicitly *or implicitly,* is rooted in a very different faith. To separate one's philosophy from its roots in faith isolates it from its most originary source and condemns it to nonultimacy. To develop a philosophy in isolation from its integration into the most profound and existentially decisive soil and context shows a high degree of responsibility, but it must be supplemented by a (no less theologically than philosophically well-informed) theory about the transformation that all abstractions inevitably undergo when they are (re)considered in light of the faith to which any thoughtful existence owes its first and final meaning.

HETERONOMY?

Many objections have been presented against the thesis that the philosophy of a Christian is not possible unless it can also function as a partial contribution to a Christian theology. I will mention here only one of these objections. Many Christian, and especially Catholic, philosophers are afraid that such a conception of philosophy submits their emancipated thoughts to the authoritative (or authoritarian) judgment of Church leaders or celebrated theologians. Instead, I would like my thesis to be understood as recognizing the important role that good philosophers could and should play within the Christian community to which they belong.

If philosophy cannot be thorough unless it gives an account of its own combination of dependence and independence with regard to theology (an account that, according to the above, should be as radical as possible, though it cannot be final),[5] the reverse is also true: to be an accomplished theologian, one must also be a good philosopher. Those Christians who are professional philosophers must be interested in those theologies that show excellence in thinking, while theologians must compete with the best philosophers in the descriptive and conceptual analysis of real life in the historical world as it is. The theologians to whom philosophers should listen must operate with the same degree of sophistication as the latter, while Christian philosophers must forge expressions of their thoughts (including their most radical ones, produced on the borderlines between philosophy and theology) that allow for conceptual and experiential debate with both Christians and non-Christians.

Since modern philosophy and theology have parted ways, many theologians have reacted to the philosophers' disinterest in theology by abandoning them to their own ideas while turning instead to philology, hermeneutics, history, archeology, psychology, sociology, physics, biochemistry, and neurology. This development has resulted in a situation where quite a number of philosophers and theologians treat one another with profound ignorance and suspicion. The harm they have thereby caused to their own search for truth is considerable. Again, versions of dogmatism, double truth, fideism, and misology have changed the normal alliance of human intelligence with grace into a polemic relationship, with all the lacks of understanding and ignorance that go with it.

After a few centuries of intermezzo, the best theologians and some philosophers of our time are doing again what enlightened Christians were doing all along for the first fifteen hundred years of the Christian era. Having learned the art of philosophical reflection from Greek philosophers, they tried to understand the truth of a faithful existence by transforming the *spolia gentium* that could be used for a converted *philosophia.* They were successful when this transformation gave rise to a thought and language of their own, well adapted to the incomprehensible but luminous mystery of well-searched and well-researched faith. If theology can do the same today, modern and postmodern philosophy may well turn out to have been another *praeparatio evangelica* whose usable elements are freed from their un-Christian errors and limitations by a faith-inspired liberation of hidden promises. For the philosophy of Christians, this implies that it will be aware of its own theological context and horizon. So long as the most plausible thoughts of philosophy have not found an appropriate place within a rightly enlightened faith, they can only be provisional, because their ultimate meaning—i.e., the meaning that permeates all other levels and elements of meaning—has not yet been discovered. At the same time, a philosophically underfed theology will remain behind in sophistication and maturity.

Christian philosophers are as responsible for the enlightenment of the Christian community as are theologians. Both need the other to be fully and radically what they are. It is a *philosophical* necessity that philosophy not shy away from questions of ultimate concern, and no theological thought can be taken seriously if it is weak in comparison with the thought of respectable philosophers. If it is true that the philosophy and the theology of a Christian cannot be contrasted in the name of sharp distinctions between nature and grace or between reason and revelation, it seems preferable to present them as interdependent disciplines that together compose the reflective form of existential wisdom that, for a very long time, has been called *philosophia.*[6]

METHOD AGAIN

Did my long (but still too short) remarks on the personal union of philosophy and faith in a Christian thinker distract us from the main question that the title of this essay promised to answer? Moreover, do those remarks not argue against rather than support the universal validity of the philosophical work produced by faithful Christians? If the role of faith in all philosophies has been determined correctly, no universally valid philosophy at all seems to be possible. Is each and every attempt to speak in the name of humanity as a whole then really doomed to fail? Are we necessarily separated, even in philosophy, by our differences in religion or faith?

I do defend that, in a sense, *each* philosophy is a form of *fides quaerens intellectum*, a thinking that is not only rooted in a form of confidence or trust or faith but also passionately, and therefore radically, dedicated to a profoundly critical and radical search for understanding the universe, the thinker, the search, and—insofar as this is possible—faith itself. This does not mean that philosophy and theology (or a theology that is rooted in its own—secular or otherwise religious—faith) can no longer be distinguished at all. Despite the impossibility of separating them by a clear-cut demarcation, theology remains primarily that part of thinking that we mobilize in talking or writing to and in the name of the faithful adherents of our own religion, whereas philosophy is the domain of a worldwide conversation among all who exchange the thoughts that emerge from their participation in the universally human search for a meaning and truth that we can share—or *insofar as* we can share them.

Christian philosophy has two faces: in conversation with those who share the Christian faith or show sympathy for it, a faithful philosopher does not have to bother about the boundary between philosophy and theology. In conversation with those who do not share that faith, however, we will try to discover a common ground with our interlocutors and keep our exchange focused on those experiences and thought experiments that can be shown to be valid for all participants without distinction. The latter, in principle worldwide, conversation does not produce exactly the same thought in all the interlocutors; not only their faiths but also the cultural and historical contexts of their reflection diversify the "generally valid" philosophy that unites them, but there is enough space for some level of agreement among them to speak of a philosophical community as wide as humanity.

That Christian philosophers are not just disguised theologians can be explained by their belonging to two communities: the body of Christ *and* the universal republic of philosophy. The latter belonging does not necessarily contradict a perfect Christian faith, but it is as difficult to remain entirely untouched by the ethos, the doubts and errors, the distance and hostilities that mark most cultures as it is impossible for a believer not to be turned and converted to the grace of faith—albeit imperfectly received. Few Christians escape from contamination by arrogance and doubts. Only perfect saints are fully faithful. Who is completely permeated by faith (with its normal components of hope and love)? Which kind of thought can be called perfectly faithful to its Christian inspiration?

The philosophy of a Catholic thinker cannot be identified as exclusively driven by the desire of a theologically correct view of the universe; it is also a critical reconnaissance of other, non-, a-, or anti-theological interpretations of existence. Before faith is alive and strong enough to take possession of a thinker's heart and brain, one is still struggling and plagued by doubts. Only a mature and deep confidence in God transforms philosophy into a possible or integral element of a philosophically satisfactory theology. The latter was the ideal of the best medieval philosophers, whereas most of us feel more often internally divided by our adherence to two communities whose dominant orientations are not easily unified in one overall horizon.

Members of Christ's body are Hebrew with the Hebrews, Greek with the Greeks, and postmodern with today's postmoderns, but they are on the way (*in via*) toward a more reconciled and peaceful life that, as far as philosophy is concerned, demands the continuation of a worldwide conversation among all seekers of the desired Same.

LANGUAGE AND AUDIENCE AGAIN

The question of the audience, which we abandoned before answering it, can now receive the outline of an answer. Although it is not possible to spell out which philosophical principles and outcomes constitute a wholly faith-free, culture-free, historically and biographically neutral system that should be shared by all who think, it is most often possible to find common ground with a determinate audience, notwithstanding deep differences that keep us apart (but—thanks to serious conversation—also together). We never speak to humanity as a whole or to some abstract "mind," "person," "ego," or "you" in isolation but always to unique persons whose singular life story and particular culture offer us an opportunity to reach them where they are while respecting how they are. Such encounters demand that, without hiding my deepest trust, I seek to come to terms with the other's convictions by means of shared interests and critical but mutually understandable questions and discourses. While learning from another whose faith differs from mine, I then hope to be encouraged by a shared pursuit beyond pluralism, while putting my hope in a hidden convergence of our ways to truth.

NINE

Sacrificium Laudis—Sacrificium Intellectus

Can philosophers offer their work to God as an expression of recognition, gratitude, reconciliation, and participation in the spirit of a sacrificial liturgy? Or, in Christian terms, are philosophers invited to the wedding of the slaughtered Lamb?

SACRIFICIUM LAUDIS

In the biblical stories about the kings of Juda and Israël, we read that, under those kings who insisted on the central celebration of the Lord in Jerusalem, idolatrous sacrifices continued to be offered on the high places and that abominable practices, such as burning one's firstborn son, were part to it.[1] We also read, however, the following words of Psalm 51:

> Open my lips, O Lord,
> that my mouth may proclaim your praise.
> You do not delight in sacrifice; or I would bring it;
> You do not take pleasure in burnt offerings.

My sacrifice, O God, is a broken spirit:
a wounded and contrite heart, O God, you will not despise.

We also read that Jeremiah, in the name of the Lord, announces a time in which all bloody offerings will be replaced by a pure devotion of minds and hearts:

"The time is coming," says the Lord,
"when I will make a new covenant
with the house of Israel
and with the house of Judah"
. . . .
"This is the covenant I will make
with the house of Israel . . . ,"
says the Lord.
"I will put my laws in their minds
And write them on their hearts.
I will be their God,
and they will be my people.
. . . .
All of them, high and low, shall know me;
I will be merciful toward their wickedness
And I will remember their sins no more."[2]

Christians believe that the promised new covenant has been inaugurated by Jesus, and they apply to him verses 7–9 of Psalm 40:

Sacrifice and offering you did not desire,
but you prepared a body for me;
with burnt offerings and sin-offerings you were not pleased.
Then I said: "Here I am—as it is written about me in the scroll—
I have come to do your will, O God."[3]

According to the letter to the Hebrews, where these verses are quoted, Jesus had to learn through suffering the obedience that is implied in the agreement of a human will with the will of God:

During the days of his life on earth, he offered up prayers and petitions with loud cries and tears to the one who could save him from the grave. Because of his humble submission his prayer was heard. Son though he was, he learned obedience in the school of suffering.[4]

That suffering was indeed a touchstone for the authenticity of Jesus' humility is clear from the anguished and twice-repeated prayer in which, on the eve of his condemnation, he urged God that "if it were possible, this hour might pass him by: 'Abba, Father,' he said, 'all things are possible to thee; take this cup away from me. Yet not what I will, but what you will.'"[5]

Although Jesus confesses that "all things" are possible for the Creator, he does not know why he "must" (*dei*) be condemned to passion and death.[6] His motivation for accepting this destiny does not emerge from any other explanation than that it is willed by God, whom he calls "Father." Without receiving an answer to the eternal question of *why* one must suffer, Jesus submits his will to that Willing, which thus is realized in Jesus' obedience to death. A human will that wills the glory of the original and all-encompassing Will transforms the situation of a corrupted world into the possibility of perfect reconciliation. To will God's Will is here the loving answer to a tragic murder that does not allow for a rational explanation. The suffering of this perfect man is the result of misunderstanding and malevolence. It cannot be deduced from obvious principles, but it must be accepted and performed, because another's Will ought to be done.

Jesus becomes the Servant and Priest of Jahweh[7] by accepting the most unreasonable but inevitable sacrifice of his life. His embrace of this fate summarizes his fulfillment of the entire Law: "Not what I will, but what You will."[8] In that will we have been sanctified through the sacrifice of Jesus Christ's body once and for all.[9]

Consequently, he could teach his disciples the following basic prayers: "Your will be done" and, anticipating the results: "your kingdom come," "your Name be sanctified."[10] Or, as Paul formulated it:

"I urge you, brothers and sisters . . . to offer your bodies as a living and holy sacrifice that pleases God. This is the worship that befits you."[11]

Christians are invited to participate in Christ's *teleiōsis*[12] by embracing the fatal destinies in which they discover themselves involved, even if it does not become clear to them why these destinies, including the massive suffering that tortures the whole of humanity, should be such as they are. What does this mean for those Christians who are dedicated to philosophy? How can the will of a Christian whose life is marked by philosophy embrace the horrors of this world in which we are placed, although much of it is neither holy nor decent? How can not only the lives but also the thoughts of such philosophers express a divine Spirit that animates and orients the universe, despite its corruption? First, however, we would like to know whether and, if so, how philosophy in general can be part of any liturgy at all.

To answer the latter question, I will first sketch succinctly how philosophy relates to the existing reality, as it is created, ruled, redeemed, and oriented toward its eschaton. This relation includes a stance with regard to God, whether this is recognized or not. The absence of an explicit reference either expresses an—as yet undecided—openness toward the possibility of God's coming or a closure of the human universe, which is then abandoned to its own devices. The scope and task of philosophy depend on the stance of the philosopher vis-à-vis the possibility of religion. A philosophy that remains open to God's interference in human thought is *absolutely* different from a decidedly autarchic kind of search. As long as philosophers agnostically hesitate to take a position with regard to faith, they delay a decision about the final meaning of their philosophy.

The second step needed is a brief phenomenology of the attitude that is appropriate to the performance of a sacrifice. Since philosophy is a work of language, I will focus here on a sacrifice that is performed in words. The letter to the Hebrews calls this a sacrifice of praise (*thusia aineseōs, hostia laudis*) and defines it as "the fruit of lips that confess God's name."[13]

The third step will then be a confrontation of the philosopher's attitude with the stance of a priest who offers a sacrifice of praise.

PHILOSOPHY

Modern philosophy began as an autonomous enterprise and developed into a sovereign mode of thought that submitted not only scientific and intellectual but also moral, political, and religious convictions and activities to its judgment. The emancipation of philosophy from religious and political tutelage is older than the modern revolution, whereas a certain but often conditional respect for religion has lasted until Hegel, but rarely have modern philosophers explicitly invoked faith or theology to prove a point or justify their work. With some exaggeration we might say that Descartes was the last philosopher who, albeit only once, at the end of his third *Metaphysical Meditation,* interrupted his philosophical argumentation by the announcement of a contemplative prayer. Not in order to invoke God's inspiration at the beginning of a philosophical work, as, for example, Augustine, Bonaventure, and Scotus did, but, after having proved God's existence, perhaps by way of closure and to exile piety and edification once and for all from the domain of philosophy, he took some time for the adoration of God's "incomparable beauty."[14]

That such a form of contemplation indeed causes an interruption in the philosophical stream of consciousness follows from the horizon within which modern philosophy thinks. Its ideal lies in comprehension of the logic according to which the universe develops, rational transparency of all that exists, and theoretical guidance for practically dealing with it. To acquire a comprehensive insight, it is necessary to mentally reconstruct the universe from scratch, i.e., from the most obvious empirical evidence together with a set of clear principles that are even more certain than immediate perceptions. Accurate perception and methodological purity are indispensable but difficult to guarantee. However, the goal *must* be realized (and here we have a human *must*) because the understanding of the universe enables us to become also the technical, medical, and ethical "masters and possessors"[15] of the facts and events that confront us in the world.

An autonomous ego imagines itself on top of some mountain, from which it can display and oversee the universe. Even before it was called such, it conceived of itself as transcendental, independent, and uncontaminated by the biases that characterize each life. Methodic abstraction would be enough to free one's real thought from all unproved beliefs. All the idols and ideologies that Francis Bacon had exposed could be avoided by sticking to the ideal of philosophical autonomy. True, several revisions of the method were necessary before Reason alone, conspiring with some indubitably given facts, could demonstrate its monopoly, but Hegel seemed to have accomplished that task by finally constructing a well-rounded system. Although Christian faith and theology still received some degree of respect, a progressive reduction of faith to philosophy seemed to prepare a complete humanization of the earth. The question of God remained alive in the background, but even Christians are no longer eager to measure the width and depth of their intellect by confronting that crucial question and similar ones. By adopting the supreme viewpoint of modernity, philosophy seems to have eliminated any role for God from its horizon.

Indeed, how could the One who is adorable and incomparable appear within the horizon of a universal display? God is neither an object among other objects nor a being amidst, behind, underneath, or on top of other beings. In order to relate to God, Ego would have to surpass or to abdicate its transcendentality in order to reach beyond the universe, instead of remaining fascinated by its coherent totality.

The professed or only methodical atheism that has become the rule in philosophy has forced the philosophers to link all human interests to other than divine realities. Because these links no longer can be understood as motivated by an orientation to God, they can only be evoked and dominated by one or more desires that point in other directions, such as comfort, fame, money, love, beauty, virtue, art, science, technology, or philosophy itself. Because such desires compete with one another, they must be reconciled according to criteria that demand rational justification. But what supreme or synthetic interest is capable of ordering the interests of these competing desires? For example, if Right, Beauty, Freedom, or Reason are celebrated as sovereign "values," they occupy the function that formerly was fulfilled by union with God. In the judgment of those who cherish the Christian heritage, all such interests become gods when they are celebrated as final consolation. We gratefully recognize the natural beauty of many desires, while deploring the ugliness or morbidity of some others, but finite desirables cannot justify absolute demands. Freedom and intelligence, science, philosophy, and theology are great, but do they deserve a liturgy of sacrifice? They cannot inspire an absolute awe that justifies utter and total dedication.

What, however, about the finitude of human persons, whose basic demands are absolute and therefore have been called "infinite"? We must indeed grant that each and every neighbor reveals absolute obligations, but we must also emphasize that these obligations are not caused by the will of those who reveal them to me. The imperative revealed in the Other's face and the awe it inspires show their affinity with the originary Desire that inhabits each one independently of all other desires. As the source of human longing, an originary *Eros* constitutes humanness as such. Desire transcends all finite desires while yet energizing them, but it feels betrayed and disappointed when it no longer is allowed to guide a human destiny.

From where do the absoluteness of the Other's epiphany and the infinity of one's own Desire come? Are they vestiges of God's precedence with regard to the created universe? The biblical identification of the neighbor with the hidden but real presence of the Infinite testifies to the double meaning of the originary Desire: what we ultimately and originally long for is union with God, but this union is not possible without welcoming human others, i.e., without living—and thus also dying—for those who happen to be part of our destiny. If we can neither choose nor destroy this most intimate Desire, what then remains of freedom, emancipation, independence, or autarchy?

The will. We are able to accept our being inhabited by a Desire that remains dissatisfied as long as we do not meet with God or have not yet learned to love our neighbor. But we are also able to resist and betray what we, as erotic beings, are. Self-betrayal makes us inauthentic and unhappy. But amazingly, we are not immune to it.

Does philosophy foster or endanger loyalty toward the deepest desire that defines us? That depends on the will that drives philosophy.

As long as philosophers allow themselves to be obsessed by the sovereign position of an ego on top of a panoramic universe, they are not open to the only One who cannot be a part of it. A panoramic position is not well attuned to the erotic transcendence that reaches out beyond the all toward a desirable One, who refers us to our neighbors on the earth. But what about a will that follows this twofold direction? Is it able, even within philosophy, to participate in a sacrifice of praise that elevates the philosopher while humbling his pride?

CAN PHILOSOPHY BE OFFERED AS A SACRIFICE OF PRAISE?

The author of the letter to the Hebrews urges his readers to "always offer to God, through Jesus, a sacrifice of praise, i.e., the fruit of lips that confess God's name," but he immediately associates another obligation with the first: "Do not forget to do good and to share with the community." Be good, share, and praise God, "for such are the sacrifices that please God."[16] Thus praise and benevolence together constitute the authentic participation in the paradigmatic sacrifice through which the friendship between God and humanity is realized.

The secret of Jesus' sacrifice was the union of his human will with the Will of "the Father."[17] Participation in this union has the same structure: Christians are urged to sacrifice not only the words of their lips but their entire body "through Christ" to God. What counts in this offering is the willing that joins the exemplary willing of the sovereign Will. In Christ, all sacrifices are gathered in a central and communal agreement with the absolute Will, i.e., with the ultimate meaning of the historical fates and facts that occur. By recognizing the sovereignty of this Will, one confesses that it is God who must be praised as being "all in all things."[18] Such willing is expressed in agreement with the factual destiny that befalls—and sometimes terrorizes—humanity. It is more ours, in its most emphatic and radical sense, than understanding, because it unites us with God, despite the deep obscurity of incomprehensible suffering. Agreeing—assenting, consenting—is free; it is not a necessity, especially in front of massive disasters or persistent injustice. It is the most original, though often blind, surrender to the all-originating Will, which, apparently, does not insist on demonstrative transparency as a condition for our most fundamental trust.

Does philosophy prepare us for such an agreement, or does its love of wisdom promote a kind of affirmation that prefers insight over piety and edification?

If a sacrifice of praise is a kind of confession (*homologia*) in honor of God's name, how can philosophical analysis and argumentation then be part of it? The stance of an all-judging ego does not seem to fit into the attitude of someone who sings the praise of a Name that surpasses all creation, especially not when such an ego conceives of itself as an autonomous and all-encompassing viewpoint. Can Augustine's *Confessions,* for example, be recognized as a philosophical work in our sense of the word "philosophy"? A will that prompts praise for an absolute Will that situates human destinies in an amazing but puzzling, splendid but also horrible world seems very different from a will to insight before and above all other desirables. Must Christians who philosophize sacrifice their desire for lucidity and the freedom of their reason to an agreement at all costs, while giving up the transcendentality of their scope?

Is the elevation of philosophy to the status of supreme tribunal a form of idolatry? One, of which one does not have to be ashamed, because it has so much more style than the primitive, archaic, or infantile idolatries that have been demythologized by modern and postmodern thought? If, despite the obscurity that surrounds the horizon of philosophy, it remains open to a Will that surpasses total comprehension, how then can a philosopher's will reach further than knowledge toward the Will that rules both light and darkness?

Opening the horizon of the philosophical universe means that the transcendent and precedent dimension of religion shows its irreducible originality. In light of the relation that links humanity to God, the universe manifests the contours of its finitude and the necessity of welcoming whatever surprises or pains us, without letting itself be enclosed by our interiorization—not even within philosophy. If an invitation from beyond the enclosure is accepted in faith, then some non-, pre-, extra-, or postphilosophical communication—perhaps in the form of a prophetic word or a liturgical tradition—may convince some philosophers that philosophy cannot fathom what escapes any systematic totality. If they then also discover that the highest possibility of philosophy lies in referring to the hidden light of a Will that provides sufficient guidance for falling in love with it, these philosophers might be surprised by the coincidence of many limitations that condition their will to insight with an obscure illumination that invites their will to an attitude of receptive attention.

Loyalty to the not only human but also "daimonic" *eros*[19] has convinced Plato and his followers that their philosophy could not stop at an analysis of the universe. Being in love refers and propels a passionate thinker to the transconceptual and metauniversal Good-and-Beautiful beyond the circle of self-conquered knowledge about the universe. During many centuries, the Platonic tradition has meditated about the radical difference between the Good and the intellectual gathering of all that is. Great minds in that tradition have pondered the infinite generosity of the One, but Christian Platonists have dared to ascertain that infinite Love involves the One itself in the kenotic drama of a sacrifice that surpasses all gods and universes by uniting the human willing with the Will of the Good itself.

Are philosophers able and willing to overcome the temptation of seeing themselves as supreme judges of all reasonable acceptance and conclusive trust? Does their philosophical thought allow their wills to set the Law? Although philosophical operations may throw some dim light on the mysteries that remain when reason has exhausted its capacities, it seems reasonable to state that they cannot produce any definitive closure within their own horizon. But this then also means that the final meaning of philosophy cannot be determined by itself and that all philosophical work is provisional and revisable. At the borders of its universe, philosophy might be urged to sacrifice its autarchy by reaching out to a dimension that is more serious and promising.

If Eros, Desire, implies affinity and a love that seeks the lovable (*philon*), the *philia* (love) of *philosophia* reaches out toward a wisdom (*sophia*) that implies, among its desiderata, an acquaintance with the limits that define the human cosmos. A wise acceptance of these limits includes a sense of the difference between this cosmos and the ultimately desired but ungiven Good, which does not or does not yet show up despite our *philo-sophical* explorations. By longing, Eros reaches further than any theory. But, being wise about a healthy and nonidolatrous longing, its most passionate attachment surpasses all understanding. As loyalty to this kind of Desire, philosophy is in touch with the Good-and-Beautiful that withdraws from all philosophers who try to capture it in the human-all-too-human network of systematic thought. The difference between the Beloved and the Known opens a space where prophetic words can be heard.

One of the tests that philosophizing Christians must undergo in order to show that—not only in their lives but also in their philosophies—they are ready to accept the one infinite Will that is lovable but also demanding lies in their struggle with instances of overwhelming suffering, for which no explanation can be found. "Jesus will be agonizing until the end of the world."[20] Indeed, we cannot stop asking why all the burning and bombing and scourging of individuals, peoples, countries, rivers, forests, and cultures occur. Not even theology has here an answer. Must we really read the book of history as a collection of love letters sent by God? When the human "Why?" remains completely unanswered, incomprehensibility hurts not only our brains but everyone's deepest longing for truth and understanding. The only guidance lies then in an incomprehensible "must" and the Will expressed in it. Is philosophy able to teach us how we should or could respond to this dark and mysterious Must? Can philosophy ever accept facts and fates that seem to seal its final ignorance? Or is this the final test—the decisive mortification—of our will to understanding?

If thinking is embedded in a life of trust and hope, as, for example, Plato's *Phaedo* suggests, thinkers draw the strength of their consent or dissent from a source that precedes and transcends their thinking. If their thought is not hopelessly abstract, it follows the decisions that motivate the lives they embrace and endure. However, agreement with such a source transforms the pride of a self-engrossed will into a form of hospitality toward revealing words. However, questioning philosophy cannot stop with its integration into any all-encompassing theology. For theologians are as much in danger of speaking from outside of the lives in which they, like others, are involved. If theology degenerates into religious studies, the critique of modern philosophy sketched above is equally valid with regard to that kind of distant erudition.

I do not see any valid argument against the integration of philosophical insights into a faith-inspired theology as practiced by a constant tradition from Justin to Cusanus; neither would I protest if an integrated reflection of the Christian community about its faith would call itself *philosophia,* as it did until the end of the twelfth century. As long as they remain separate, however, philosophers and theologians should join their scholarship and reconnect, in a postmodern way, with the premodern tradition of integral contemplation. Emancipation, freedom, rights, rigorous analysis, and enlightened universalism cannot and should neither be slandered nor neglected, but the contemplative blending of veneration with insight-seeking desire, as practiced by the Capadoceans, Augustine, Anselm, Bonaventure, and their more recent heirs, reminds us of an unfinished—and interminable—task: How can we—now in a postmedieval and postmodern way—integrate philosophy in a sacrifice of praise that transforms intelligent lives and works into a faith-inspired approximation of the first—creative—Word? Instead of asking whether philosophy can produce texts for a sacrificial liturgy, we might ask whether philosophers are willing to join the chorus of confessors at such a festival.

However, a contemplative renewal of philosophy cannot be a reason for abolishing the practice of a *relatively* independent and *provisionally* autonomous philosophy. In the first place, because philosophical analysis and composition need a moment of distance from complete absorption. It must, for example, continue to test the power of transcendental perspectives on the universe, and it can be humble while trying to discover how far the human intellect reaches in the reconstruction of creation.

A second reason why philosophy should not be totally absorbed by mystical contemplation lies in the fact that it has become a preferred mode of universal communication at the service of humanity as a whole. It is not necessary to believe in the existence of an independent system of natural reason, but it would be a terrible loss and an incentive for many wars, if we abandoned our attempts at forging a worldwide and peaceful conversation, despite our division into cultures, languages, and religions. That all such attempts remain deficient because, as yet, we do not possess a universal language, faith, or systematic thought is not a reason for forming linguistic, cultural, philosophical, or religious ghettos nor an excuse for imposing one version of universality on all the interlocutors. Universality of words and ideas flattens. It cannot be the supreme criterion for truth, because it neglects the concrete multiple uniqueness of all singular persons and other realities. But it realizes a necessary though insufficient condition for worldwide possibilities of communication, i.e., for an unlimited field of eloquent peace and growth in mutual understanding.

What philosophers must sacrifice is the tempting claim of being able to pronounce the final judgment about truth and goodness. If the universality of an all-encompassing view can neither replace nor wholly swallow all prayer and sacrifice, philosophy can join them by offering amazed and amazing commentaries on that kind of devotion.

TEN

Philosophy as Mediation between Faith and Culture

Mediation is needed when two or more parties are engaged in a conflict that they cannot overcome by their own efforts alone. Are Catholic faith and the dominant culture of our epoch engaged in such a conflict, and is philosophy capable of playing a role in its resolution? It is my task to offer you some thoughts about this question, as a contribution to the teaching and research that we accomplish in the service of our communion in Christ, of cultures in which we participate, and of humanity as a whole in this critical period of its history. My limitations are obvious: the culture in which I have been educated is European, the society in which I participate is North American, and the philosophy and the theology with which I am acquainted are "Continental." Of course, the Western perspective on culture and the world has to be surpassed by a much wider vision, but life is much too short for learning all we should know about faith, culture, philosophy, and theology to anticipate the universal perspective that, we hope, will be realized in the future.

As for the conflict between faith and culture, it is obvious that the Church is in deep disagreement with much of the dominant culture with regard to social justice, the arms race and war, the death penalty, sexuality, marriage, and abortion. The Church also continues to be opposed to capitalistic occupation, colonization, and exploitation; totalitarian perversions of communism; and philosophies that foment atheist, skeptical, and antihumanist behavior. If reconciliation or compromise between faith and the dominant culture is possible, and if philosophers are asked to mediate between the parties, what could we then expect from them? In my remarks about this question, I will restrict myself to philosophers who are also Catholic (or, rather, to Catholics who are also good philosophers), because I suppose that all of us who are meeting here are such persons or else want to know how such persons think. This restriction has two sides. In the existential conduct of their lives, Catholic philosophers identify with one of the parties: *faith*. As philosophers, however, they are not only well acquainted with the history and the actual situation of philosophy, but they also sympathize with several trends of the contemporary culture. Catholic philosophers are therefore qualified to act as go-betweens, which is one condition of mediation. Whether they fulfill all other conditions has yet to be seen. Does their simultaneous participation in faith's eternal life and in the history of philosophy prevent them from having the distance necessary for good judgment and diplomacy regarding both parties? Perhaps—but who then are better qualified to mediate?

I will use the word "philosophy" to indicate a historical phenomenon that marks our lives insofar as we, through our profession, belong to a particular, historically grown, worldwide society or "republic" of philosophers who, despite numerous and deep differences, feel and show a certain degree of solidarity.

With the word "faith" I do not indicate what contemporary analytic epistemology means when it speaks about "belief" or what Plato and Aristotle called *doxa,* but instead I mean the appropriate response of an entire human person to God's invitation to recognize God as the loving creator and redeemer who invites us to participate in God's own trinitarian life. *Credere in Deum* means that one confides one's entire life to the Creator, who wants to adopt us as sons and daughters in the unique Son, Jesus Christ, whose Spirit grants us participation in the eternal love that unites the Father and the Son. A faithful Christian participates in God's eternity. This is why "eternal life" is synonymous with a life that follows the way of Jesus: even before personal resurrection, we live, in historical modes, the eternal life of God's sanctification.

Faith implies not only gratitude, absolute and self-aware dependence, a fundamental humility, and indestructible hope but also the profound and cordial affirmation of certain truths—an affirmation that expresses itself in affections, symbols, and appropriate formulations. Besides narratives, prayers, hymns, prophecies, sermons, and poems, faith certainly generates communicative and explicative propositions or beliefs, but theoretical or properly theological elaborations emerge only in cultures where the human intellect has introduced a reflective and theoretical climate, at least among a group of well-educated persons.

To be faithful does not imply that one is good at definitions or reasoning, but if some Christians are also philosophers, they can neither remain naïve about God's revelation nor build an impervious wall between their own philosophies and the implicit or explicit theology they profess by reflecting about their own faith.

Regarding the contribution that Catholic philosophers can offer to a *modus vivendi* of their faith in dealing with the contemporary culture, I will begin by sketching some features of Western culture as it has developed in the last centuries, while giving special attention to the self-expression of this culture in philosophy. Then I will turn to some crucial tensions between our faith and our culture in order to consider the possibility and some conditions of a fruitful mediation. To finish, I will give some examples of mediation.

TODAY'S WESTERN CULTURE

The description of a particular culture is always a difficult task, especially when one tries to characterize such a huge and complex universe as "the contemporary culture" is. The result can hardly be more than a highly selective and simplified picture of a particular society in which the portrayer feels at home. Such a selection is marked by the sociological, historical, and philosophical perspectives of the author's cultural milieu. Personal and epochal elements thus play an important role: our descriptions of past cultures are always anachronistic, whereas contemporaneous descriptions have too little distance to clarify what really is happening. The task becomes even more difficult when the cultural homogeneity of a huge society—and we are talking here about several continents—has receded, to be replaced by a sort of meta- or superstructure that gathers several, rather different, cultures within its horizon.

In the following attempt at sketching some characteristics of today's Western culture, I will emphasize the idea of *freedom*—an idea that has also been an ideal. With the greatest fervor and hope, this idea(l) has been celebrated—and to a certain extent realized—as the practical (i.e., morally and politically relevant) aspect of *Reason,* which, in its theoretical use, has displayed its power in *science* and *philosophy.*

Although the word "postmodern," which dates from the end of the nineteenth century, has recently had much success among intellectuals, it is not so clear what it means besides its negative implications, according to which the modern era is terminated and a new era has begun. Modernity is not yet quite dead, however—indeed, modernity and its ideal of freedom are still very powerful, although many of us, especially in Europe, share the feeling that modernity has been agonizing for more than a century—and the expression "*post*modernism" is not eloquent enough to give us an orientation for the future. Many philosophers probably think that Nietzsche marks the threshold between modernity and postmodernity because of his radical critique of truth as such. I prefer to see Hegel as the ambiguous end of modernity, because of the radical pluralism that, from Feuerbach to Derrida, has changed philosophy into a chaotic multitude of orientations and styles, neo-isms, and star-led epigonisms. Postmodernity is not the name of a new culture but rather the provisional title for a period of transition in which the Western civilization, through many experiments, exaggerations, and self-criticisms, tries to find out which direction it—and the entire world—should take.

In order to situate our culture with regard to our faith (and the eternal life into which this faith has introduced us), we need to look back to the past of both our faith and our culture, because we cannot predict their future and have too little distance from our present involvement to grasp its secrets. Memory and the risky attempt of summarily characterizing the past centuries must help us to understand the cultural determinations of our life. Even the choice of freedom as the main feature of our culture confronts us with a task that surpasses our forces, because the modern conception and practice of freedom cannot be cut off from its roots in the Greek and Roman civilization or from its many renaissances during European and American history. Moreover, a serious phenomenology of Western freedom presupposes a synthesis of disciplines besides philosophy, such as sociology, political economy, art history, theology, and so on, which cannot be mastered by one person. Therefore, I will restrict myself by focusing, from a mainly philosophical perspective, on the ideal of freedom as it has been celebrated during the last four centuries.

To understand the modern culture, one could begin by rereading Descartes' *Discourse on Method.* Through its description of the method that philosophy should follow after the rejection of its scholastic traditions, that text gives a succinct idea of the theoretical emancipation that the greatest thinkers from Descartes and Spinoza, via Leibniz, Locke, and Hume, to Kant and Hegel tried to achieve. Although Descartes and others still insisted on the philosophical task of acquiring wisdom,[1] their philosophical program was modeled after the new sciences, whose results seemed to promise indubitable, transparent, and universally controllable truth. All opinions and authorities—including the beliefs and mores of the dominant traditions—had to be distrusted. The goal of human wisdom was to make man the "master and owner" of nature,[2] and although Descartes, in a short passage of his spiritual exercises called "Metaphysical Meditations," takes some time to adore God,[3] the ancient and medieval idea that philosophy has intimate links with prayer and contemplation disappears completely from the history of philosophy, and a place is made for a moralistic concentration on willful praxis, scientific theory, and masterful technology.

The autonomy of human thought itself is proclaimed the unshakable bedrock on which philosophy should build. Humanity has emancipated itself from all other guidance than the one provided by its own observations and the light that a pure and universal reason sheds on the universe that is displayed for all.

Modern freedom implies also a unified praxis, insofar as it liberates its ethical and political program from political and ecclesiastical authorities who try to impose views that are not recognized as universally valid and rational. Locke, Rousseau, Kant, and Hegel, but also Marx, Nietzsche, Sartre, and Foucault have focused their endeavors on the conditions and consequences of freedom as praxis, while the social and political developments of the last centuries cannot be understood without seeing that collective and individual freedom has been the main driving force of world history. Nationalism, the liberation of former colonies, proclamations of "human rights," and democratization have changed the social patterns that rule our consciousness and the motivation of our behavior. All of us are born and educated in an ethos of liberty; we cannot tolerate any kind of servitude, unless we freely choose to assist or accompany others who need us, but even then we are reluctant to call ourselves "servants." Instead, we prefer other words, such as "philanthropy" or "professional behavior," to mask the social inequality that might be associated with "serving," and expressions like "*servus servorum Dei*" are considered misplaced in our society.

Whether our society really is democratic remains to be seen, but as an ideal, "democracy" has certainly become a shibboleth. Its foundation is generally seen as lying in the idea of human *rights*, understood as equally valid claims of all human individuals to the goods that are necessary for everyone's realization of basic needs. Freedom and right have become two sides of the one characteristic principle—Reason—that defines the practical and theoretical ethos of the modern era. Right is the normative aspect of everyone's freedom as faced by all others, while duty is understood as the claim through which a person's own freedom—as practical reason—obligates itself. Right and duty are the names of two inseparable and radically identical sides of modern freedom, not only in its moral and political concretizations but also in its theoretical—scientific and philosophical—practice. Philosophy is the work of an emancipated thinker who has the right to examine and judge all opinions, beliefs, and faiths. Autonomy of thought has become the first commandment and the first right of philosophy.

Initially, this right included the belief that the correct use of reason alone, supposed to be universally present in all normal individuals, sufficed to find or reconstruct the truth. Later, however—and this shift might be seen as one aspect of the transition from modernity to postmodernity—this trust or faith in reason itself was shaken, and the distinction between rationally free behavior and personal preferences became blurred. Sartre went so far as to claim that the liberty of human "existence" creates the programmatic "essence" that rules each individual life.

In the average culture, freedom became a synonym for the private ability to choose what I want, and morality was reduced to the rule that I must allow all others to choose as freely as I myself from the goods that are available. The privatization of freedom and rights on all levels of life and culture resulted in difficult relations between individuals and the guardians of collective interests. Both individualism and patriotism (the individualism of singular nations) became virulent, causing many kinds of colonialism, war, and genocide. In philosophy, "pluralism" became a catchword for describing its scattering into a multiplicity of currents and schools that hardly allow for a common denominator.

Some of the reasons why the initial optimism about freedom changed into a loss of faith in the modern program lie in the fact that none of the systems produced by modern thinkers was entirely convincing (every system was quickly followed by new attempts at refoundation, on which new systems were constructed), but the main reason was that faith in reason itself came under attack. The names of Marx, Nietzsche, Freud, Heidegger, and Wittgenstein stand for a long and still ongoing search for more originary sources that motivate and feed our thinking and, in this sense, lie deeper than (or "precede") reason. What drives our passion for thinking, what populates our imagination, what performs and refigures our experiences, what are the real goals that obsess our frenetic activities, what causes our crises and malaises, and so on? The social structures, the unconscious desires, the language games in which we are caught, the obscure pathos that drives all our desires, the corporeal and political conditions of our lives and the traditions that have shaped us are studied through old and new metaphilosophical sciences, through which we hope to discover the roots of thought. Positivism and historicism were nineteenth-century forms of this metaphilosophy, but in the meantime, psychoanalysis and linguistics have found more acceptance, at least among philosophers. It is obvious, however, that philosophy, though very interested in learning from the sciences, cannot abdicate in the face of scientific diagnoses that try to impose their partial perspectives as if they could give access to ultimate conclusions.

The sociological, linguistic, biological, psychoanalytic, and historical findings of the last three centuries have profoundly shocked and shaken an older trust in the uncontaminated purity of human reason and free will. Instead of protesting against all forms of dethronement or enthusiastically accepting a total determinism of human activity, philosophers now must reconsider the entanglement of reasonability in all kinds of conditioning that are disclosed as belonging to our corporeal and psychical existence in a nonangelic world.

The multifaceted portrayal of human existence at the mercy of so many powers has reinforced the dissemination that resulted from the individualistic scattering of modern freedom, mentioned above. Which thinker possesses the synthetic ability needed for a philosophical diagnosis of all the suggestions that are offered by the human and natural sciences? If such a person exists, he or she will have answered the question of whether desire, language, social structures, the unconscious, or any other power or cluster of powers is fundamental enough to replace the principles and grounds of the reason on which prepostmodern philosophers counted to project their systems. In any case, a simple dismissal of all the influences that have been unveiled, as if they were only marginal, is not a sufficient response to the drastic changes that, for more than a century, have transformed our milieu. The traditional conceptions of reason and freedom—and, for that matter, of human nature—are in need of a thorough rethinking. At the least, the modern concept of freedom must be transformed into a more receptive, less "egoic" or "selfish" concept, one closer to the medieval *voluntas ut natura* than to a *liberum arbitrium*. At the bottom of personal freedom lies a fundamental ability to accept and assent, preceded by a "natural" orientation that can only be affirmed and appropriated or hated—but not eliminated as long as one exists.

Doubts and suspicions about the primacy of reason have a longer past than postmodern and modern philosophy. Even during the heyday of German idealism, Herder, Goethe, Hamann, Baader, Jacobi, and others denied that reason could found itself, and the philosophical tradition of the *heart* as more profound than reason stretches from Plato through Augustine, Bonaventure, and Pascal to Blondel and Levinas.

In contrast with a cordial orientation that transcends or precedes the particular conditions of human thought and praxis (such as language, libido, etc.), the absolutization of those conditions creates contemporary idols that philosophy desires to overcome. As long as we are not able to show how such conditions situate but do not abolish freedom, we remain caught in uncertainty about our historical situation. It does not help to condemn this situation as relativistic or skeptical or to accuse certain thinkers of indulging in sophisms, instead of practicing ourselves the ascetic work of careful analysis and refined description. It is even possible to find promising elements in the pluralism of our situation, insofar as it is accompanied by a healthy distance toward the ideal of a dogmatic doctrine that could and should be held by all. Totalitarian states have tried to impose such doctrines on their citizens, but fortunately they have failed miserably. We seem to have learned how to coexist and cooperate with one another without agreeing on theses and theories. Apparently, we can treat one another decently despite disagreements about propositional manifestations of the truth. The many disappointments that all the philosophies since Hobbes and Descartes have generated justify a healthy skepsis with regard to the autonomy of human thought, and we have discovered that each philosophy has a secret that escapes our attempts to capture it in the concatenation of our sentences. Behind each theoretical unfolding there is a hidden source of inspiration: the particular spirit that inspires and continues to animate the thoughts and words in which a thinker tries to say what motivates his heart.

Indeed, each philosophy is not only a historically concrete and unexchangeable version of the quest for truth; it is also inspired by a *spirit* of its own. Or, as we may cautiously venture to say: each philosophy is rooted in and nourished by an ultimate or most originary and decisive stance-in-motion: its most fundamental *faith*. No philosophy can be radically neutral if philosophy is wholly *serious*, i.e., if it asks and studies the decisive questions of human life itself. Thinking cannot begin without at least a burgeoning hope, i.e., without a wager about the ultimate meaning not only of thinking but, more fundamentally, of human existence as such.

The clearest example of such a philosophical faith is Hegel's explicitly stated "faith in reason," which was the only condition he asked his audience to bring to his courses when he gave his inaugural addresses in Heidelberg (1816) and Berlin (1818).[4] Not all philosophers share Hegel's conception of reason, nor his faith in it, but for every coherent philosophy, one can discover and describe which fundamental stance and perspective dominate its entirety. At the roots of each authentic body of thought lies a source that is characterized by a particular mode of affection (a fundamental mood or attunement, a radical desire, and a faith) from which imaginative and conceptual patterns emerge in interaction with the patterns of the surrounding world. "Beneath" and "before" the experiential and conceptual network that constitutes a philosophy, its spirit emerges from the thinker's "heart." Not only does each human heart have its own reasons, coming from a deeper depth than logic; it also stands and desires, moves, hopes, and trusts or distrusts in a unique way of its own.

These statements, which—I hope—you will consider to be a hypothesis more or less worthy of consideration, demand a change in the customary conception and method of philosophy. They seem to me the only possible way of explaining why none of the philosophies produced since Descartes' *Discourse on Method* has been able to fulfill the program he proposed to all future philosophers. The thoughts of all philosophers, including the modern ones, have been influenced not only by historical circumstances and traditions, linguistic, imaginative, affective, and conceptual patterns but also—and on a deeper or, rather, the deepest level—by an ultimate trust, which we can call "faith" in the broad sense of the word that precedes all beliefs.

Globally speaking, the "faith" of modernity is "faith in freedom": freedom of behavior and freedom of thought. Modern and postmodern philosophies are sophisticated celebrations of humanity as source and summit of a humanistic universe. God was not always excluded from this universe—from Descartes to Hegel, a certain faith in God remained the cornerstone of the great monuments of thought—but the relevance of God was measured by the standards of humanity's liberation from political and ecclesiastical humiliation. The absolutization of the human perspective resulted in a finitist conception of God, and the competition between this idol and Humanity led to the proclamation of God's death. The ensuing atheism restricted the possibility of a dialogue between Christians and "post-Christian" atheists to a debate about religion as favorable or harmful to human maturity.

What I said about the spirit, the heart, and the faith of serious philosophers can also be formulated in another, more Nietzschean terminology. All philosophies and ideologies are driven by a characteristic *pathos*. Thinking and believing bring the "stance" of the thinker to the verbal surface by passing through the conceptual networks that structure the thinker's lived experiences. We are what we think. *And* we cannot be identified with our theories. The analysis of the affective constellations that motivate and guide the exploration of roots and sources is another of the urgent tasks that the changing climate of philosophy imposes on today's philosophers in their own domain.

As for the cultural pluralism and relativism that threaten to replace all reflection by the blessing of well-formulated opinions, perhaps we may understand them as challenges to a (re)discovery of sources that lie deeper than science and theory. If so, then they are not necessarily signs of despair or decadence but rather invitations to a more profound philosophy than the modern ideologies.

A second promise might be found in our pluralism, if we may interpret it as a manifestation of each singular person's *uniqueness* as expressed in the style of his or her words, behavior, painting, singing, thought, or faith. In the practice of philosophy, this shows in the singularity of each and every original thinker and in an authentic recognition received from others. The secret of a philosophy is in the first place the individuality that speaks in it, even after the philosopher's death. A good reader hears an inimitable voice, which cannot be reduced to the skillful features of the systems it proffers.

A most interesting and, for our purpose, particularly relevant development in recent philosophy is the rediscovery of its dialogical character. After the obsessive egocentrism of a panoramic and objectifying Cogito in all its empiricist, rationalist, and transcendentalist versions, we have finally awakened to the reality of our always already being involved in relations with others that cannot be reduced to elements of centralized and all-encompassing thematization. The ideal of an ego that mentally embraces all beings, including other persons and God, has been recognized as a violent and falsifying illusion. You, he, she, and I myself transcend and escape all horizons, contexts, and universes. All that can be thematized as part of the world and its history, all contents *about* which we can speak, are subordinate to your, her, his, or my own speaking that displays the universe for some ego's consciousness. *Speaking and listening* form the basic and ultimate "horizon" or "space" within which You and I find ourselves caught before, during, and after each and every thought we produce. Or rather: *listening* comes *before speaking,* because nobody is able to speak without first being addressed or called. Speaking begins always as an answer to an address that provokes me. Speaking, as the core of language, is always already responding after listening and, as a new speech, a new provocation that elicits an answer from someone other.

The dialogical character of all language has become central in a promising part of contemporary philosophy and is waiting for further investigation. The overwhelming sympathy it has generated in the general public shows that it will have its consequences in philosophy and theology. Instead of remaining a series of monologues, philosophy takes again the form of a conversation. Independently from the content, the addressing—e.g., in the forms of presenting, proposing, or offering—constitutes the structure on which all possibilities of understanding depend. The to and fro of our communication conditions all social and cultural phenomena. Neither traditions nor faith would be possible if they could not count on real interlocutors who confront one another. Unaddressed propositions or theories would be as dead as musical scores that are never performed.

The dialogical drama that gives life to a culture is, of course, crucial for the internal and external unity and diversity of all communities. It is the very condition of togetherness, sharing and exchange, education, reflection, and critique. After the modern universality of identical egos, we return to the communicative pluralism of unique persons who share, in unrepeatable modes, their communal destiny.

GOD

If I insist here on the modern celebration of individual freedom, it is to counterbalance somewhat the greatest failure of postmedieval culture: its progressive elimination of God from the practical and theoretical scene. Much could be said and resaid about the secularization, the agnosticism, and the atheism that characterize the public life of the Western society and the theories of many quite famous philosophers. Even many of our children, nephews, and nieces show how little the God we adore impresses or attracts them, even when they are fervently engaged in social activism and service to the poor, the homeless, and the persecuted. Is it possible that God hides more than ever behind the faces and the needs of our fellow humans? Is it even possible that the concentration on human rights has drained the energy away that formerly was canalized by devotion to God and the saints?

The activities of Amnesty International, Doctors without Borders, and innumerable other philanthropic and charitable foundations, the massive protestations against war and global exploitation, the great generosity of so many persons in the battle against hunger and homelessness, and so on show much more than an idealistic movement for realization of human rights. More than respect for right, they express a spirit of compassion and humble dedication to all who suffer wherever they are and a widespread aspiration for worldwide friendship. Even in the United Nations, this solidarity is operative. No wonder that philosophers have begun to think about ways of surpassing the idea of equality in rights—which always has a tendency to individualize and oppose—by more convivial patterns of solidarity. We see a revival of studies on *philia* and renewed efforts to reconcile care for individuals with dedication to the communal good. In the context of a desire for mediation between Catholic faith and mainstream culture, we must answer the question of whether God's absence from our culture is only a semblance. If it is true that "God is there where charity and love are practiced" (*ubi caritas et amor, ibi Deus est*), as we sing when we commemorate, together with Christ's suffering, the suffering of all who participate in his Passion, is God then not visibly and tangibly present in those who humbly suffer and in those who alleviate their suffering?

The second remark I would like to make about the atheism of our culture concerns the difficulty of postmodern men and women to sense the difference between the finite universe and the infinity of God. Since the earth on which we live has become a tiny stone in a spatiotemporal universe that we can embrace through the endless horizon of our thought, God's absolute otherness and infinity has become even more incredible for many than it was for the ancient Greeks, who could see infinity only as limitlessness and imperfection. Is the ensuing lack of faith only the fault of the atheists, or have we, the Church, failed in faithfully testifying to the wonderful circuminsession of God's incomprehensibly infinite sovereignty and the amazing but lovable humility of God's *kenosis*?

Some observers consider the actual state of philosophy decadent or bankrupt. If they are also theologically well informed, they might add that such decadence is the consequence of our "original" sinfulness but that this result does not condemn the philosophical enterprise as such. They might refer to a doctrine according to which philosophy, as one of the noblest activities made possible by human nature, despite its being threatened by sin, has remained able to know basic tenets of the truth we need, even if its views must be adjusted by those who profess faith in God's revelation. But before we enter into a theological discussion about human nature, sin, grace, and faith, let us restate our main question regarding the philosophical mediation between faith and culture.

CONDITIONS OF A PHILOSOPHICAL MEDIATION BETWEEN FAITH AND CULTURE

If Catholic philosophers are asked to mediate between faith and culture, they will answer that their task can only be a limited contribution to coexistence or reconciliation. In the first place, they will emphasize that it is faith itself—and consequently the people of God as a whole together with its leaders—that, in the Spirit of benevolence and wise discernment, must respond to those voices and practices of the existing culture that seem to distort or deny the truth that makes us free.

In the second place, Catholic philosophers will point out that they are doubly biased, because they are not only members of the Church but also citizens of the Republic of philosophy. Indeed, it is not true that philosophers just speak from ivory towers, as isolated thinkers who consult only their own human nature and its inherent intelligence. As little as theologians can speak in the name of God's revelation without passing through the historically grown wisdom of the apostolic and ecclesiastical traditions, philosophers can speak in the name of a natural wisdom that is contained in creation without appealing to the traditions of the historical community to which they belong. As modern and postmodern persons, they are not able to think like an imaginary Adam without past or future history but only as children of their time and heirs of many ancestors. As simultaneously belonging to both the Catholic Church and the existing culture, their philosophy necessarily expresses some sort of union between faith and culture, even if it is a tense or schizoid one. True, they are free to differ from certain opinions of both institutions, but one can neither belong to the Church without agreeing with the faith core of its orthodoxy nor to Philosophy without sympathizing with its generally practiced methods and recognized conquests.

The third limitation Catholic philosophers will underline is that their perspective is philosophical and thus not encompassing enough to represent the perspectives from which scientists, artists, social workers, psychologists, sociologists, neurologists, economists, politicians, and so on could illuminate the actual situation and the minds of philosophers, theologians, and ecclesiastic officials.

If Catholic philosophers all the same are urged to mediate, they must not only decide how they can be fair to both the concrete and often tainted history of the Church and the culture of the society in which they live, but they must also self-critically look at their own philosophy. As Christians, they will want to express their faith in the most authentic way of which they are capable, while, as philosophers, they will try to save as much as possible of the thoughts that have impressed them in conversation with their fellow philosophers. However, they must criticize what, in the light of the truest faith and thought of which they are capable, seems to be a pseudofaith or superstition within the Church or a false and wrong *doxa* in the surrounding culture and philosophy.

Can Catholic philosophers be fair at all? Since faith is a deeper and more originary source of knowledge than reason, they are primarily on the side of the Church, even if they cannot agree with all the opinions or imperatives that its leaders support. Moreover, philosophers who are acquainted with the main developments of the last four centuries are not simple servants of ecclesiastical or scholastic theologies but—if they are good at their job—respectful and respected members of a thoughtful community that gathers all philosophers of the world. This community has its own dominant ethos and beliefs. A certain form of solidarity with this republic is inevitable, even if it creates tensions with Christian loyalty to the Church.

The Catholic philosopher is one of the meeting points where the tension between Church and contemporary culture is felt intensely as a serious problem, one caused by the task of living eternal life *in hoc seculo*. Consequently, Catholic philosophers cannot consider themselves to be freestanding judges who are neutral with regard to the tensions we are concerned about. They are loyal to both worldwide institutions, but in different ways and degrees. But they remain responsible for the individual way in which they receive and integrate the lessons they learn in them. If they are asked—or experience it as their God-willed task—to mediate between faith and culture, they must reflect on the union of faith and culture in their own person. Eternal life, inspired and kept alive by the Spirit of Christ's mystical body and the heritage of the civilization in which they are at home, meet in this personal union.

With regard to the dominant culture, Catholic philosophers have as many rights as all other philosophers to speak in their own name (which is always in the name of certain traditions that have been integrated by individual philosophers), but they are unable to speak as thinkers who lived in the fourth century before Jesus Christ or the thirteenth century after. However, their loyalty to the Church plays a role other than their solidarity with the philosophical community. It is not true that the latter rejects all authority. The loudly proclaimed autonomy of modern philosophy has never been achieved, and it is easy to show that all associations of philosophy have their own orthodoxies, canonical texts, authorities, fora, consecrated heroes, and exclusions. Philosophy is never completely neutral but always particular in its questions, preferences, selections, methods, and solutions. Reason and experience are never merely "natural" but always already educated, formed and reformed by particular teachers and traditions. Moreover, philosophy has never been an individualistic product of isolated thinkers, but each time again it is an original transformation of borrowed elements gathered in a characteristic mode. None of the great philosophies is therefore a *philosophia perennis*, if this expression means that we simply must repeat what is already known. Some oeuvres remain exemplary, however, and we may hope that all great philosophies in some way converge toward the one and ultimate truth.

As philosophers, Catholic thinkers cannot acquiesce to any form of naïveté, unless they first submit all the important elements of human life, including their own, to the most thorough reflection of which they are capable. Even from a purely philosophical (or "natural") perspective, no Catholic philosopher can be taken seriously if she does not ask and answer the question of how Christian faith influences her philosophical research and teaching. Sophisticated intellectuals cannot barricade themselves behind the walls of an obligatory or dogmatic philosophy. Their thinking habits inevitably extend to a critical analysis of the faith that guides their lives. Since, as Catholics, we know that our faith is a gift of grace while at the same time being the most fundamental stance of our existence, we also know that an adequate understanding of this faith presupposes a combination of theological and philosophical elements, which, as such, are neither revealed nor proven by the best professors of the world. Because of their being grounded in faith, Catholic philosophers cannot keep themselves altogether out of theology, although they may persist in trying to discover the exact demarcation between their philosophical and their properly Catholic and theological knowledge. Because rootedness and radicality imply involvement and risking the meaning of one's life, they cannot bracket their deepest commitment—faith—when they practice philosophy earnestly.

To what extent must Catholic philosophers share the dominant assumptions cultivated in the republic of "free" thought? If modern faith in human autarchy is the touchstone for being respected as a philosopher, this seems to contradict clearly the humility that is essential for Christian trust and gratitude. Or could one defend that such a proud manner of thinking can be justified as a hypothetical and provisional position that ulteriorily should be "sublated" by integration into a humble adherence to the wisdom of Christ? Such a transition from a more or less hypothetical philosophy to an intelligent form of faith could, for instance, make it necessary to study thoroughly certain assumptions or results of self-declared atheists, to see whether some of their assumptions would fit into an irreproachable theology. The criterion that rules such an examination lies then in Catholic faith, which Catholic philosophers cannot choose to ignore. They must be aware of the extent to which their Christian faith shapes their attitude toward the philosophy that is produced in the secular culture, and they cannot silence the question of how their participation in God's intertrinitarian life permeates their own historical existence, including their heart and their intelligence, and consequently their philosophy and theology. If grace is not separated from the rest of a human life by an impermeable wall, it is not possible to separate authentic philosophy from authentic theology. But if a philosopher declares that his criterion, even for philosophy, lies in an orthodox formulation of Catholic faith, will he then not be ridiculed or excluded from all philosophical associations that respect themselves? Has such a person lost his philosophical honor?

Although Catholic philosophers are not called to be also specialists in theology, a certain expertise in "the search of faith for understanding" cannot be missed for their *philosophical* self-understanding. This does not mean, however, that they must accept the theology of particular theologians, as if such were the most adequate formulation of the truth about God and humanity. Especially the logical, epistemological, methodological, anthropological, cosmological, biological, metaphysical, and hermeneutical elements that are assumed in the available theologies are not *de fide*. For the most part, they are elements that theology has borrowed from the Hellenist, Roman, and European cultures it has absorbed during its history. The use that the Church has made of the various theologies that emerged in different periods of its history does not convert them into the quintessence of faith, but they belong to historical concretization of this faith. Although philosophers recognize in these theologies characteristic conceptualities of bygone epochs, they still can admire the ways in which the faithful thinkers of those epochs incorporated borrowed elements into their own explanations. It does not mean, however, that today's philosophers or theologians should canonize any former theology or philosophy, as if they could put their faith in theories instead of trusting the Spirit of Jesus Christ as preached by the Apostles and their successors in the service of the Word.

The distinction between faith itself and its theoretical clarifications must be emphasized, especially in a time of cultural crisis and shifts. In such times, the underlying spirit or faith of the dominant culture is changing or has already changed, which undeniably expresses itself in the figures of philosophy that emerge from that culture, although philosophers often trail the artists in registering the moral and spiritual shifts that have already occurred.

That philosophy has been changing continually since the end of the eighteenth century and that we are still in the midst of experimentations and blind alleys is an experience shared by many philosophers, who, at the same time, agree that we cannot return to the methods and doctrines that were accepted before the Enlightenment. Consequently, Catholic philosophers who today meditate about the faith of the Church can no longer embrace outdated theologies insofar as these imply elements of outdated philosophies. The kind of research we need today must show that the Spirit of Christ is able to speak new languages without forgetting the old ones. Every cultural shift demands a retranslation and renovation of theology and of the philosophy implied in it. Since our faith is a gift of grace, a philosopher cannot expect that it can be fully comprehended, but as a Christian, one must try to acquire orientation and clarity in the borderland where philosophy meets with theology and its underlying faith.

As participants in the republic of philosophy, Christian thinkers are acquainted—and to a certain degree in sympathy—with the general mentality that rules the philosophers' ethos. Probably we should rather use here the plural "mentalities," because of the dissemination that characterizes the actual situation of philosophy, but if it is true that freedom still can serve as a simplifying denominator, we might resort to this ideal to delay an analysis of that complicated dissemination.

Christian philosophers, and especially Christians who are well versed in both philosophy and theology, are the Church's greatest chance of mediation between her faith in the Holy Spirit and the spirit of the existing culture, which expresses itself in today's philosophies. Indeed, Christian thinkers should be able to fulfill the two contrasting functions that are united in their own person: to speak as advocates of a philosophical culture that no longer can be characterized as Christian and to be inspired by the Spirit that animates the Christian community. By urging them to enact what they are, the Church grasps the opportunity to be informed about the meaning and motivation of many people who stand inside or outside—and sometimes on both sides—while at the same time learning how to express its faith in an experiential and conceptual language that is more appropriate to our own time than to outdated ones. Before evaluating some influential philosophies, the Church thus has the opportunity to listen and to recognize some of her own desires and truths in their search for the truth.

"NATURAL REASON" AND THEOLOGY

If we are called to mediate, we cannot avoid the question of what we, as Catholics and philosophers, should think about the distinction between philosophy and theology. If we define philosophy in the modern way as a kind of thinking that restricts itself to the experiential and logical capabilities of the human essence or "nature," or—to use a *pars pro toto*—if we restrict philosophy to the work of "natural reason," without borrowing anything from the typically Christian experiences that are generated by God's grace or the Christian heritage that has become an integral part of world history, then we might be inclined to define theology as the thoughtful discipline that bases itself explicitly on revelation, while confining philosophy to a part of humanity that supposedly is neither touched by grace nor by sin.[5]

According to a certain theology that dominated Catholic thought from the sixteenth to the middle of the twentieth century, the boundary between philosophy and faith would lie between natural reason, whose relative autonomy in relation to grace would then be theologically justified, and faith, as a divine virtue through which God gives us a "supernatural" enlightenment. This theology maintained that the purity of a (human) *natura pura* was a sufficient basis for the rational discovery of God as first and infinite, perfectly perfect, and all-powerful Being. The standard explanation of the difference between a philosophy produced by natural reason and the distortions of philosophy for which atheists were made responsible was then sought in an unintelligent or sinful obscuring of the possibilities that natural reason possessed. Some Catholics tried to show that they made a better use of natural reason than non-Catholics by retrieving old demonstrations, for which they even found support in ancient philosophers. Their advantage was that faith already had revealed to them what they had to discover through a relatively autonomous reason.

Today, however, few Catholics are convinced that they themselves or any other philosopher can demonstrate God's existence in any rigorous sense of generally accepted logic. Fideism is a real danger. But if nature is sufficient, how then can we explain that God has gradually disappeared from philosophy? Are all of us less intelligent than earlier thinkers?

The concept of a "pure nature" might be a valuable tool for the Christian theology of grace. Indeed, it is difficult to justify the distinction between creation and redemption if we cannot make a distinction between nature and grace or between the essentially human level of experience and reason, on the one hand, and the level of God's undeserved grace that has been revealed to us in the history of Israel and Christian faith, on the other. If it is true, however, that God has never been unloving or ungracious in dealing with creation, it is hardly possible for us to know what exactly a human nature would be and will and feel and do if it were abandoned to itself by God's Grace. If God created the world as part of a design that leads up to divinization, then all nature from its beginning, and especially the nature of God's human "image," is enveloped, heeded, addressed, provoked, and permeated by grace. In other words: if Abel, Enoch, Gideon, and Samson excelled in faith (Hebr. 11:4–5, 32), then it is not clear where exactly the threshold between nature and gracious illumination lies. But if we do not know what characterizes "pure" nature, then we cannot know either what such a nature can know on its merely "natural," or as yet ungraced, level.

From a Christian point of view, philosophy cannot be defined as a natural knowledge in the sense of a *natura pura*. This theological concept remains abstract (which does not necessarily take away its utility in certain contexts); it cannot be described as a concrete situation that would ever have existed on its own, untouched as well by human sin as by God's plan of salvation.

All human existence has been damaged by sin and influenced by grace. As a historical reality, philosophy is the concrete history of human thinking that tries to find the best way toward truth while continually dealing with the omnipresence of God's gracious presence and the temptations of sin. From a merely philosophical standpoint, i.e., from the standpoint of someone who does not explicitly believe in Jesus Christ as God's revelation, the categories "sin" and "grace" do not belong to the philosophers' daily vocabulary, although a certain affinity with the Christian experience of grace and sin might emerge from their experience of evil and gratitude-without-addressee. In any case, the history of modern and postmodern philosophy cannot be interpreted as an illustration of the knowledge that human nature as such can acquire "on its own," because such a nature, free from all grace and sin, does not exist and has never existed in history. Some elements of any given philosophy seem natural, other elements might be sinful, and still other elements illustrate the incognito presence of grace. Perhaps we may interpret the latter as "postfigurations" more or less analogous to the biblical and "pagan" prefigurations of faith in Jesus Christ from Abel and Noah until Job and Plato. A theological diagnosis of contemporary philosophy may try to sort out how these elements can be isolated and how they together form a typical constellation or "figure" of human thought, but for our purpose the decisive question is not what an abstract and ahistoric nature or essence is able to find out but rather what kind of mentality or *spirit* speaks or expresses itself in the historical phenomena and "figures" of today's philosophy.

In any case, we cannot identify the normal product of "natural reason" with the results obtained by the modern and postmodern heroes of thought from Descartes to Heidegger and Levinas. On the one hand, they would seem to have produced more than nature is able to produce on its own, for example when they plead for universal equality, social justice, and self-forgetting dedication to others, whereas, on the other hand, they have found less truth than those theologians expected who declared that natural reason is able to prove the existence of God and the immortality of the soul. Are their failures consequences of sin, and are their successes due to aftereffects of the Christian tradition? Were Catholic philosophers who thought that they could demonstrate the existence of God less sinful or more natural? Or did they borrow from the grace of their faith, which not only freed but also elevated their intellect?

Until recently, many Catholic philosophers have followed the advice that they should have taken recourse to the theology of Saint Thomas and the philosophical elements that his genius was able to integrate in his theology. There they could find philosophical "proofs" of God's existence and of some kind of eternal life for human souls. In the meantime, it has become obvious (1) that the distinction between nature and grace remains an abstract distinction between elements, none of which has ever concretely existed in isolation from the other; (2) that it is impossible to resuscitate a past philosophy without rethinking *and thus thoroughly transforming* it into expressions of a different culture; and (3) that no philosopher is able to produce a vibrant and contagious thought unless he or she is passionately engaged in a radical experiencing and thinking that Augustine, Bonaventure, and Pascal would call cordial. In this respect, it deserves reflection that, among modern philosophers, Malebranche is one rare example of an eighteenth-century philosopher who can compete with Hume or Rousseau. He was not afraid of overstepping the borders between philosophy, faith, and theology. Neither were, in the twentieth century, Maurice Blondel, Gabriel Marcel, Simone Weil, Romano Guardini, Karl Rahner, or Henri de Lubac.

From these three statements—combined with the thesis that philosophy, to be serious, must be rooted in faith and inspired by an originary spirit that gives life and blood to its experiential and logical arguments—it seems to follow that Catholic philosophers cannot separate their faith from their philosophy. If it is true that a philosophy without faith is without source, without heart, without spirit, and without pathos, then the thoughts of Catholic philosophers either draw their inspiration from their basic faith or they belong to a game without serious consequences. But if philosophers let themselves be guided by faith in Christ, are they not theologians rather than philosophers? My answer lies in a combination of the following remarks.

1. All other engaged philosophers are as biased as we are because of their basic faith, which might be more in line with the culture in which they feel at home than with the faith tradition that has formed within the Catholic Church thanks to innumerable saints and prophets, mystics, poets, musicians, architects, theologians, and priests.

2. If, *for Catholics*, philosophy becomes again an integral part of theology, we will have rediscovered the meaning of *philosophia*, as it was practiced and named from Justin and Clemens to the end of the twelfth century, especially by Saint Augustine, who understood the "love of wisdom" as love of Christ, whom Saint Paul calls "*sapientia et fortitudo Dei*" (1 Cor 1:24).

3. Catholic philosophers cannot be thorough and radical if they do not understand how their philosophy relates to their faith. Such a metaphilosophical understanding presupposes enough theological knowledge to position their philosophical findings in relation to the universe of explicitly faith-fed thought that mirrors the gnosis of eternal life on earth.

4. The authenticity of Catholic philosophers depends on their originary stance and on the spirit that shows in their thoughts. In speaking to non-Christians, we do not always have to emphasize the typically theological topics that are alien to our interlocutors, but we cannot engage in a very thorough conversation without bringing to the fore the primary sources of inspiration on which we rely.

5. Mediation between faith and culture involves Catholic philosophers in authentic eloquence on two fronts: while representing the eternal life lived in the community of Christ for the benefit of their philosophical friends, they present those friends to the Church as worthy to be heard. Both directions of their attention urge them to seek a wise discernment regarding the two solidarities that constitute their personal and professional identity.

PROBLEMS AND EXAMPLES

To give a few examples of the mediating role that a Catholic philosopher could play, I do not consider it useful to repeat here all the slogans that are used in superficial condemnations of today's culture. Labels like "hedonism," "materialism," "secularism," and "relativism" are too shallow and unfair to do justice to the best philosophers of post-Renaissance times.

In their search for an appropriate answer to the modern challenge, the leaders of the Catholic Church have condemned a host of ideas and practices that were promoted by brilliant and less brilliant minds. Since Galileo, they have persisted for centuries in condemning the natural and hermeneutical sciences through which modern scholars tried to emancipate their very sophisticated knowledge from ecclesiastical tutelage. Not only the astronomical and biological knowledge of Catholic theologians but also their exegetical and historical scholarship was paralyzed by official declarations until deep in the twentieth century. Likewise, the Church has tried to stop the recognition of individual rights as principles of social and political organization. Pius IX, the pope who began as a liberal, is well known for having condemned the entire liberal movement that, during the nineteenth and twentieth century, would conquer the European intelligentsia, and the condemnation of modernism by Pius X confirmed the reactionary direction that the Catholic bureaucracy had taken. For a long time, popes and bishops seemed not to like the idea that all individuals had inalienable rights on earth, although they continued to see them as fully responsible for their obedience or disobedience to the obligations they imposed on the details of the priests' and the lay people's daily most intimate life.

Catholic philosophers were admonished to stay within the limits of a theologically outdated doctrine, and future priests were educated with the help of handbooks that offered a pallid extract of neoscholastic thought while ridiculing the monumental philosophies that expressed and influenced the spirit of the contemporary culture. It is only in the twentieth century that Catholic philosophers began discussing the philosophies of Hume, Kant, Hegel, and Marx, whereas a promising retrieval of their own pre-Thomistic traditions by a "New Theology," prepared by Maurice Blondel, Joseph Maréchal, Gabriel Marcel, Roman Guardini, Simone Weil, Karl Rahner, and Henry de Lubac, is still in the making. Theologians who, in the early twentieth century, applied the renewal of hermeneutics and exegesis to their explanations of the Biblical sources were silenced or removed, and it is less than a century ago that they were slowly allowed to do what now has been recognized as their theological duty in teaching and research.

Similar examples of a condemnatory attitude toward the advances of modern culture can be given with regard to legal, economic, political, sexual, and philosophical questions. The *aggiornamento* of Vatican II was a necessary step toward the liberation of faith from its confinement to an outdated, typically Western, and half-medieval, half-modern culture. But in the meantime, very important decisions of that council have been boycotted by Roman and other authorities. Those of us who are old enough to have experienced the transition of a pre–Vatican II Church to its aftermath know what I mean. That the quintessence of faith, as God-given access to eternal life in union with God, cannot change follows from its divine character, but that it cannot exist without any alliance with historical cultures follows from the Incarnation of God's Word. Faith as such does not have a history, but all its practical, imaginative, verbal, and symbolic expressions are human and—within certain limits—mutable (although this does not exclude continuity over time). This law of faith and culture does not imply that all existing cultures are good or acceptable as they are. On the level of culture itself, criticism and self-criticism must accompany all originality. They are motors of change, which in the best of cases is a form of amendation, amelioration, purification, or salvation from decadence and death. What can the faithful do to support this task? What can and must faithful philosophers do to share in the mediation between the Church they love and the culture that has transformed the manners of their lives? As members of the historical republic of philosophy, they feel a certain sympathy with the best intentions and attempts of past and present philosophers, which have resulted in admirable—albeit still imperfect and sometimes sinful—monuments of freedom, right, depth, and clarity.

Condemnation does not seem the best method, not only because it sins against the rhetorical device that we should "capture the benevolence" of our audience but also because it alienates rather than converts the condemned and misses an opportunity to learn what small or large aspects of the truth their proposals or protests might hide. To follow the inspiration of the Spirit might sometimes call for stern condemnation—for example, when empires or dictators, through their infernal machines of monstrous destruction, crush entire populations and propagate the worst perversions—but to show how peaceful and just and enjoyable a life in the Spirit of Jesus is, the Church should be the best example of a fraternal community in which only the deepest respect and sincere benevolence are considered normal, together with their natural sequels: a sisterly and brotherly form of listening and speaking, blessing, advising, serving, demanding, sharing, confessing, pardoning, and encouraging. Instead of condemnations, less negative approaches seem more appropriate to foster our own and others' conversions, for instance, with regard to the modern conception of knowledge and individual rights.

Fortunately, the first philosopher who was elected pope, John Paul II, has done much to reconcile the modern sciences and the recognition of human rights with the ethos of the Catholic Church. This time, the errors of the Inquisition and Pius IX with regard to freedom of science, conscience, and religion were justly, though only implicitly, condemned. One cannot say, however, that the Church has already found a satisfactory balance with regard to modern freedom or that Christian faith and the Western culture have achieved a peaceful symbiosis. Catholic intellectuals, and especially many philosophers among them, still feel a habitual suspicion about the attitude of their leaders. To be fair to those philosophers, we must realize that the Inquisition and the *Index Librorum* have expired only recently, that it is only a few decades ago that the prophetic gestures of John XXIII have occasioned a new Pentecost, and that the resurgence of authoritarian phenomena after Vatican II has not reassured them that a respectful approach toward well-intentioned disagreements will become the universal standard of behavior.

Indeed, even without direct condemnations, one can create an authoritarian climate by peremptory declarations without paying attention to serious advice or by silencing theological debates—for example, about the ordination of women. Unilateral declarations without preliminary debate or answering questions are an efficient strategy for promoting stupidity and preventing communication—not to mention mutual love—between authorities and thinkers. Insisting on obedience does not help if one cannot convince the faithful—including philosophers—that dogmatic declarations are firmly rooted in the biblical revelation and its apostolic tradition or in the insights of "natural" reason. With regard to the latter, many philosophers would consider themselves more competent than those who are too busy with governance.

Docility is often demanded in the name of Christian obedience, but many Catholics see a rejection of well-motivated professional advice without presenting intelligent counterarguments as a failure in leadership. According to some observers, there is a puzzling incongruence between the rather positive attitude of today's Church toward the introduction and amelioration of democratic customs and institutions on the level of national and world politics, on the one side, and the distribution of power, jurisdiction, and debate maintained by its own bureaucrats, on the other. For example, few leaders are willing to discuss the question of whether the universal priesthood of Christian men and women demands more participatory and representative institutions than the ones that are officially recognized. Discussion is often stopped or prevented with the argument that "the Church is not a democracy." I believe that I speak also in the name of many others when I answer defenders of the status quo by proposing the following four theses.

1. It is not possible to treat adult men and women in the same way as one treats children, as if they have not been brought up in a climate of shared deliberation, consultation, and negotiation from their childhood on. Many of these women and men are performing similar political functions with responsibilities that are comparable with or that even surpass that of many priests. The beautiful virtues of humility and benevolent listening should not be reserved for them alone.

2. The Church is not a political institution, because it is not built on power but rather on trust and love. The Spirit of Christ gathers a community in which each member of Christ's body washes the feet of all others—and not merely once a year.

3. The entire question of whether a political organization should be either a monarchy, an oligarchy, or a democracy sounds outdated, because all big communities are necessarily organized through a combination of the three principles of government that *together* guarantee the unity, the plurality, and the totality of the assembled people through mediating institutions. A fortiori, the worldwide community of Christ is neither a monarchy, nor an oligarchy or democracy, but pope, bishops, priests, and laypersons have their appropriate roles and responsibilities for the benefit of the whole.

4. The organization of the Church as communion in the name of Christ and under the impulse of the Spirit should not only be an example of absolute respect for each person's innate freedom but much more: a fraternal service, *diakonia*, or *ministerium* driven by the love that enjoys and promotes each and every other's unique destiny and irreplaceable originality as an absolute and infinitely worthy presentation of God's divinity.

If these theses are defensible, the first question is not whether the Church should imitate either the political organization of some contemporary state that euphemistically calls itself a democracy or rather the structure of an absolute monarchy. The basic question regards the social practice of a spiritual fraternity emulating and considerably surpassing the best social and political organizations in heeding each individual's irreplaceable contribution to communal life. A generous recognition of human rights is a minimal condition for the ecclesiastical realization of worldwide *agapē*, which, however, far surpasses any right by approaching all fellow humans as friends, by friendly giving and humbly receiving brotherly corrections, by initiating and leading conversations, inviting and correcting advice, and fostering each one's contribution to the flourishing of Christ's body in the service of humanity.

Not every detail of the modern theories about human rights is true and perfect, but as a whole, the legal praxis and theory of the secular society has developed an impressive plea for a basic level of togetherness on which all moral, legal, economic, and political decency should be founded. In the name of faith, we are grateful for the movement of liberation and universal recognition as one of the great gifts modern culture has given us, despite its perversions and antireligious errors. Many heroic women and men of our age, including priests and a number of bishops, have testified, not only in declarations but also by sacrificing their lives, to their absolute respect for the sacred rights of the exploited and persecuted and the all-overriding necessity of their liberation from oppression by pseudo-Christian powers within and without the Church. Granted that it is still necessary to refound and amend the available theories about social justice and liberation, neither theologians nor philosophers can mediate between faith and cultures of oppression otherwise than by trying to persuade everyone involved that each and every unique human destiny is more lovable than the entire universe. If we, who believe in God's incarnation, cannot show that the *communio sanctorum* realizes peace by universal dedication and all-inclusive dialogue, our preaching about love sounds horribly false.

It is a disaster that the culture of the Western hemisphere, despite its recognition of some essential rights through social legislation on the national scale, has betrayed its proclaimed ideal by strengthening, centralizing, and globalizing the capitalistic exploitation of the poor and weak who, in non-Western countries, are forced to enrich the West. The incredible wealth produced by the poor for the pleasures of the wealthy few is devilish, the clearest manifestation of evil in this world. Can there be any reconciliation between this kind of capitalism and a faithful community of Christ?

In the course of the twentieth century, the Catholic Church has become one of the leading players in the struggle for universal respect toward every human individual, strong or helpless, born or unborn, innocent or criminal. Shouldn't we now also think of new ways to institutionalize the ideal of friendship in Christ, internally as well as externally, in religious but also in economical and political domains? Here lies a task for Catholic philosophers, albeit a limited one. Together with specialists of the social sciences, we must do more than show why respect is necessary, which experiences lie behind it, and how denials of universal rights lead to contradiction and disaster. We must also rethink and surpass the great traditions of social thought, including the ancient and medieval ones, in order to discover the cultural and institutional conditions of a coherent friendship of all with all in a worldwide fraternity.

GOD

The greatest challenge to which our faith must seek a response remains certainly the widespread atheism of our culture. We must recognize that a world without the true God is a terrifying night—at least as terrifying as the flaming outbursts of nationalistic, imperialist, or fundamentalist terror. Clearly, philosophers have a mediating role in this respect. By scrutinizing the affective and logical motivations of contemporary disbelief, they can prepare a better diagnosis, but their main contribution lies in the passionate search for the Good itself, whose infinity transcends all beings while illuminating and permeating them.

Some might say that God's light will not shine soon again because of God's anger caused by our systematic destruction of men and women, boys and girls, born and as yet unborn babies, homes, villages, towns, nations, forests, and animals, and—even more radically—of air, water, and soil. They may be right, but couldn't we also surmise that God became disgusted with too much empty, superstitious, idolatrous, presumptuous, self-deserving, and pedantic talk about the holy Name? Or that God wanted to give humanity an opportunity to recognize not only its own freedom, strengthened by its scientific and technological discoveries, but also its temptations and possible perversions?

God's hiding is painful, but faith in God remains convinced that the divine omnipresence-in-compassion guarantees that everyone who seeks also finds, albeit by way of an endless seeking for the Unique One who cannot be found otherwise than as the always-Sought. Even if many call God's hiddenness "absence" or even see it as a definitive farewell, it remains possible to pray—for example, in the silence of a listening, waiting, and calling trust that God will come as the One who always has been. If the general culture is mourning and then forgetting the God who shaped the Western civilization, we know that for God two thousand years are only a day and that we must testify to God's reappearance in figures and cultures we do not yet know, although we already are touched by God's whispering, to which we awkwardly respond with questions and provisional answers.

Philosophers are probably not the best interpreters of prayer, although they at least could describe and analyze what prayer means for those who pray, but it is certain that our perspective on the universe, as seen from the supreme viewpoint of *Ego cogito,* radically changes when we accept the universe in gratitude as the basic gift and word that we, in hope, can dedicate to the Origin from which it comes. From the standpoint of prayer, the world is no longer the panorama of a supreme thinker but a given that mediates between God and us.

If God is still present in our culture, we must seek the phenomenality of this presence in the motherly, fatherly, sisterly, and brotherly words and deeds of all who are driven by sincere compassion. If it is true that the best of modern liberation is oriented toward a new kind of universal fraternity, this movement may console us as a new attempt to realize the second commandment, which is equivalent to the first. If loving God is demonstrated by service to the poor and weak, then not only many Christian volunteers but also all other dedicated nurses, doctors, social workers, pilots, administrators, truck drivers, and so on testify to God's compassion against the injustice of hellish greed and imperial arrogance, which are unfortunately too much acclaimed, even by Christians. Contemporary philosophy is full of philanthropic intentions and arguments, but the world has been changing too quickly since the premodern era of world history to offer us readymade blueprints for reform. Even the legal and political programs based on modern philosophy from Hobbes to Hegel and Marx are outdated, although the practices of nationalism, imperialism, and capitalism are more virulent than ever. The organization of the United Nations is a beginning that hopefully will develop into a worldwide *entente cordiale,* but its future is uncertain and, as are all human endeavors, ambiguous. As a political organization, it might repeat the conflicts between medieval emperors and the Church. It may also die under the attacks of some pseudo-Christian or anti-Christian Empire. Or it may develop into a public parallel of the religious future that was symbolized when John Paul II prayed in Assisi together with the leaders of other religions. Whatever happens, faith includes hope and patience. God's presence cannot be destroyed, not even by the cruelty of world wars and global exploitation. But our hope is not sincere if we condone worldwide injustice by withdrawing into philosophical speculations about theism and atheism, without showing the mysterious coincidence of God's existence with human passion for the most universal and most intimate justice and friendship worldwide.

NOTES

1. THAT WE ARE A CONVERSATION

1. Cf. Aristotle *On Interpretation* 17a27ff., 19b5ff.; *On the Soul* 430b26–27.

2. For Levinas's distinction between *le Dire* (saying) and *le Dit* (the said), see his *Autrement qu'être ou au-delà de l'essence* (La Haye: Martinus Nijhoff, 1974), 6–9, 58–65, 195–201.

3. See chapter 3 of this book and Adriaan Peperzak, *Thinking: From Solitude to Dialogue and Contemplation* (New York: Fordham University Press, 2006), chapters 2 and 3. The speaker can also address him- or herself. The soliloquy is even a favorite genre among philosophers, but even this manner of proposing or negotiating thoughts and proposals or propositions creates an interlocutory distance between (my) *I* and (my) *me.*

4. Cf. Adriaan Peperzak, *Elements of Ethics* (Stanford, Calif.: Stanford University Press, 2004), 102–105, 207–220.

5. Cf. Martin Heidegger, *Unterwegs zur Sprache* (Pfullingen: Neske, 1959), 22ff.: "*die Sprache spricht.*"

6. Cf. Peperzak, *Elements of Ethics*, 153–163.

7. Cf. Peperzak, *Thinking*, chapter 3.

8. Cf. Adriaan Peperzak, *To the Other: An Introduction to the Philosophy of Emmanuel Levinas* (West Lafayette, Ind.: Perdue University Press, 1993), 19–30; and Adriaan Peperzak, *Beyond: The Philosophy of Emmanuel Levinas* (Evanston, Ill.: Northwestern University Press, 1997), 53–71.

9. Cf. Peperzak, *Beyond*, 125–127; and Peperzak, *Elements of Ethics*, 124–138.

2. ON THE UNITY OF THEMATIC PHILOSOPHY AND THE HISTORY OF THOUGHT

1. The real, lived time of the production is not identical with the time it takes to read the final organization of the text that concludes its genesis, but

both times involve a movement of thinking that we, as re-producers, must produce while trusting our own memory and anticipation.

2. Cf. Plato *Symposium* 206b–e.

3. THE RELEVANCE OF INTERSUBJECTIVITY FOR FIRST PHILOSOPHY AND THE HISTORY OF PHILOSOPHY

1. For the meaning of "first philosophy" (*prōtē philosophia,* cf. Aristotle *Metaphysics* 1003a21–32; 1016b19–30; 1026a10–32; 1060b31; 1061b5, 10, 32; 1064a28–b14) and its subsequent interpretations from Aquinas to Husserl, see *Historisches Wörterbuch der Philosophie,* vol. 2 (Darmstadt, 1972), col. 726–729.

2. Cf. Plato *Symposium* 206e–209e.

3. For a more elaborate defense of the thesis that thematic philosophy forms one indissoluble whole with the history of philosophy, see Adriaan Peperzak, *System and History in Philosophy* (Albany, N.Y.: SUNY Press, 1986).

4. As far as Heidegger is concerned, cf. *Sein und Zeit,* §26, where the fundamental level of intersubjectivity is characterized through the words "so-wie," "auch," and "mit."

5. Cf. Adriaan Peperzak, *Thinking: From Solitude to Dialogue and Contemplation* (New York: Fordham University Press, 2006), 18–22,135–137.

6. Emmanuel Levinas must be mentioned here, because his oeuvre is the first plea for a recognition of the foundational importance of interlocution in philosophy. See Adriaan Peperzak, *Elements of Ethics* (Stanford, Calif.: Stanford University Press, 2004), 98–137.

7. Cf. note 4.

8. Cf. Emmanuel Levinas, *Totality and Infinity: An Essay in Exteriority* (Pittsburgh, Penn.: Duquesne University Press, 1969); and Peperzak, *Elements of Ethics,* 98–137.

9. Cf. Plato *Symposium* 206b–209e.

10. I call the anonymous doxa here a "quasi-we" to distinguish it from the communal *we* that results from an examining conversation.

11. Cf. Plato *Politeia* 515c–e.

4. EDUCATION: RESPONSIVE TRADITION

1. G. W. F. Hegel, *Gesammelte Werke* (Hamburg: Meiner), 18:18.

2. Aristotle *Metaphysics* 12.7 (1072b3–4).

3. Cf. his *Differenz des Fichteschen und Schellingschen Systems der Philosophie* (Jena, 1801), in *Werke* (Frankfurt: Suhrkampf, 1970), 2:15.

5. PHILOSOPHY: WISE ABOUT FRIENDSHIP?

1. Cf. Adriaan Peperzak, *Elements of Ethics* (Stanford, Calif.: Stanford University Press, 2004), 77–79, 84–88.

2. Cf. Adriaan Peperzak, *Thinking: From Solitude to Dialogue and Contemplation* (New York: Fordham University Press, 2006), 18–23, 134–137.

3. See also chapter 1, above.

4. On Heidegger's *Mitsein*, see *Sein und Zeit* §§25–27.

5. Cf. also Adriaan Peperzak, *Philosophy between Faith and Theology: Addresses to Catholic Intellectuals* (Notre Dame, Ind.: University of Notre Dame Press, 2005), chaps. 14–15.

6. Cf.—from a different perspective—Martin Heidegger's often repeated dictum "*Die Sprache spricht*" (Language speaks), explained, e.g., in *Unterwegs zur Sprache* (Pfullingen: Neske), 22ff.

7. Cf. Peperzak, *Elements of Ethics*, 98–100, 110–111.

8. Aristotle *Nicomachean Ethics* 8.3–4 (1156a6–1157b5).

9. If all friendships can be characterized by the simultaneity of these three aspects or levels, the difference between noble and ignoble or good and bad friendships must be sought in other aspects, but let us drop this question for now.

10. Cf. Peperzak, *Philosophy between Faith and Theology*, 163–165, 190–193.

11. Maurice Nédoncelle, *Vers une philosophie de l'amour et de la personne* (Paris: Aubier, 1957).

12. Cf. Descartes, *Discours de la méthode*, sixième partie, AT VI:62: "et ainsi nous rendre comme maîtres et possesseurs de la nature."

7. PHILOSOPHY VERSUS FAITH?

1. Cf. Pierre Hadot, *La philosophie comme manière de vivre* (Paris: Albin Michel, 2007).

2. Cf. Adriaan T. Peperzak, *The Quest for Meaning: Friends of Wisdom from Plato to Levinas* (New York: Fordham University Press, 2003), chaps. 8, 10, 11.

3. Cf. G. W. F. Hegel, *Gesammelte Werke* (Hamburg: Meiner), 18:6, 18:18.

4. Some aspects of the relations between faith and reason are also studied in Adriaan Peperzak, *Reason in Faith: On the Relevance of Christian Spirituality for Philosophy* (Mahwah, N.J.: Paulist Press, 1999), esp. chap. 8, pp. 89–104.

5. Hegel, *Gesammelte Werke*, 18:6, 18:18.

6. Cf. Gregory of Nyssa, *La vie de Moïse*, ed. Jean Daniélou (Paris: DuCerf, 1968), 210–213.

8. THE UNIVERSALITY OF A CHRISTIAN PHILOSOPHY

1. G. W. F. Hegel, *Gesammelte Werke* (Hamburg: Meiner), 18:18. For the meaning of "faith" in this context, see note 3, below.

2. See Adriaan Peperzak, *The Quest for Meaning: Friends of Wisdom from Plato to Levinas* (New York: Fordham University Press, 2003), 7–22.

3. "Faith," in the originary sense evoked here, does not necessarily coincide with the explicitly religious faith of a confessional community such as the Christian faith, which, in this chapter, is accepted as paradigmatic. How exactly the two meanings relate to each other is a difficult question that will be studied elsewhere. See also the preceding chapter and Adriaan Peperzak, *Reason in Faith* (Mahwah, N.J.: Paulist Press, 1999).

4. See Adriaan Peperzak, "How Natural Is Reason?" in *Philosophy and Theology* 21, no. 1–2 (2009): 179–198.

5. See chapter 7.

6. Cf. *Historisches Wörterbuch der Philosophie*, vol. 7 (Darmstadt: Wissenschaftliche Buchgesellschaft, 1989), col. 623–656.

9. *SACRIFICIUM LAUDIS—SACRIFICIUM INTELLECTUS*

1. Cf. Psalm 50:14; Heb 13:15; Augustine *De Civitate Dei* 10.5.

2. Jeremiah 31:31–34, quoted in the letter to the Hebrews 8:8–12.

3. Heb 10:5–7.

4. Heb 5:7–9; cf. 2:9, 14, 17–18.

5. Mk 14:35–36; cf. Mt 26:39; Lk 22:42; Jn 12:27, 18:11.

6. Mk 8:31; Mt 16:21; Lk 9:22.

7. Heb 4:14–5:10.

8. Mk 14:36.

9. Heb 10:10.

10. Mt 6:9–10; cf. Lk 11:2.

11. Rom 12:1.

12. Heb 2:10; 5:9; 7:11, 19, 22, 28; 12:2, 23.

13. Heb 13:15.

14. Descartes, end of the third *Metaphysical Meditation*, AT VII:52; IX:41–42.

15. Descartes, *Discours de la Méthode*, sixième partie, AT VI:62.

16. Heb 13:15–16.

17. See notes 2–11.

18. 1 Cor 15:28.

19. Plato *Symposium* 201d–212c.

20. Pascal, *Pensées*, in *L'œuvre de Pascal*, ed. Jacques Chevalier (Paris: Pléiade, 1936), 1060, n. 736 [87].

10. PHILOSOPHY AS MEDIATION BETWEEN FAITH AND CULTURE

1. Cf. Adriaan Peperzak, "Life, Science, and Wisdom According to Descartes," in *The Quest for Meaning: Friends of Wisdom from Plato to Levinas* (New York: Fordham University Press, 2003), 123–148.

2. Cf. Descartes, *Discours de la Méthode,* sixième partie, AT VI:62.

3. Cf. Descartes, AT VII:52.

4. G. W. F. Hegel, *Gesammelte Werke* (Hamburg: Meiner), 18:18.

5. Cf. Adriaan Peperzak, "How Natural Is Reason?" *Philosophy and Theology* 21, no. 1–2 (2009): 179–198.

INDEX